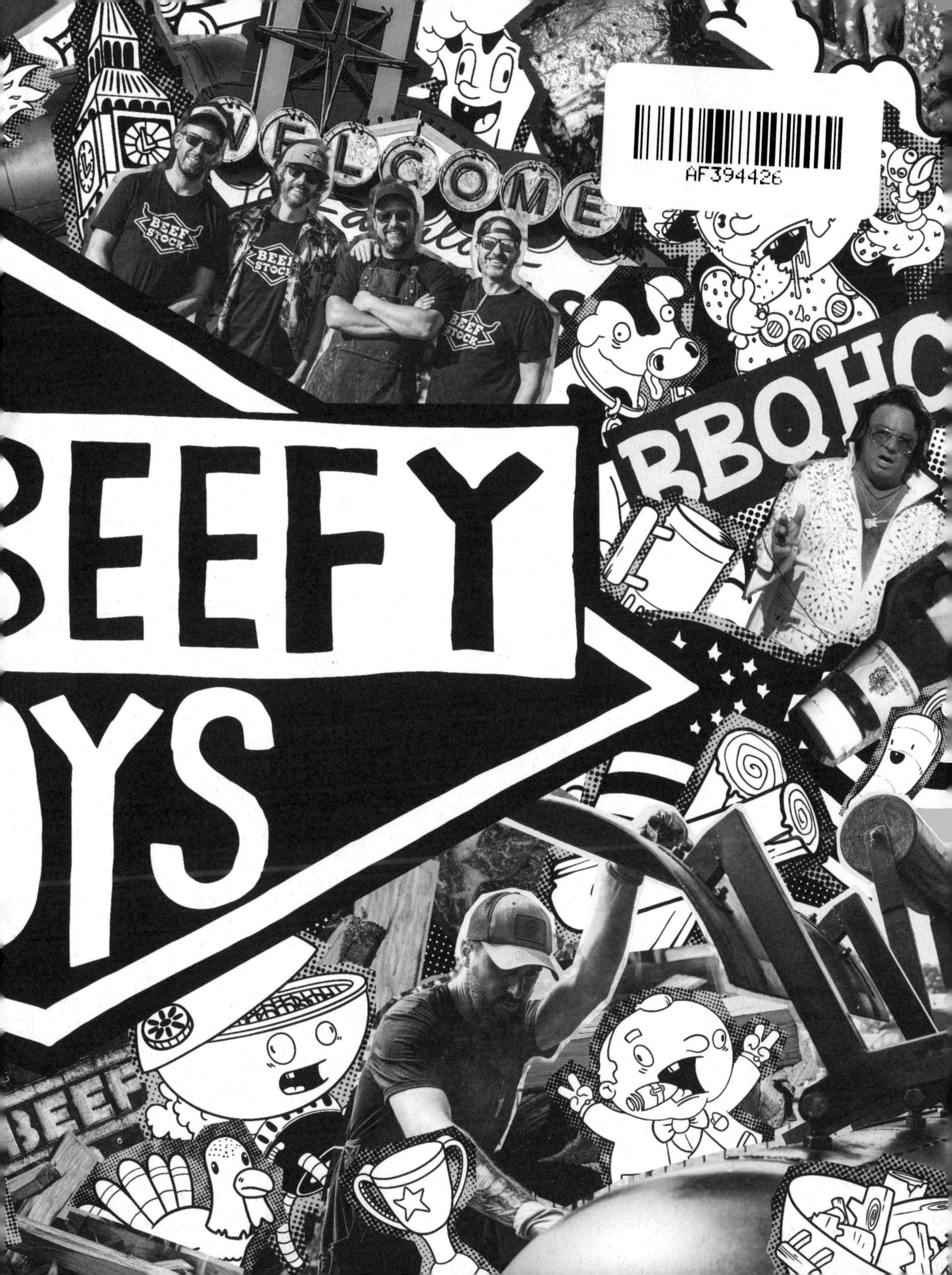

BEEFY
OYS
BEEF STOCK
WELCOME
BBQHC
BEEF
AF394426

"OVERRATED AND UNDERCOOKED."

Some bloke on Tripadvisor

THE BEEFY BOYS

GREAT BRITISH BBQ

Written by
ANTHONY MURPHY

Photography by
PETER LOWBRIDGE

Designed by
JOANNA MURPHY

Illustrations by
ALAN QUARTERMAIN

Quadrille

CONTENTS

Hello. We are The Beefy Boys.

**There is a high chance you are reading
this because:**
**A. Someone bought you this book for Christmas
or your birthday because they had no clue what
else to get you but knew you liked food.**
**B. You found it in a bargain bin somewhere,
picked it up on a whim, and this opening
paragraph is already making you regret your
life choices.**
**C. You bought our first book, read it, and
somehow still came back for more.**

Either way, this is the part where we are supposed
to introduce ourselves. We are The Beefy Boys. All
four of us used to live normal lives. Two of us were
DJs at a pretty terrible nightclub. We also ran the
nightclub, which is why it was terrible. One of us
was a gas engineer. One of us was a runner for
daytime TV charity-based antiques show *Flog It*.
We had all known each other since childhood and
our teenage years, and then one day, we had a
BBQ that got really out of hand. So out of hand
it changed all of our lives forever.

After cooking for some friends and family and
getting a bit too cocky about how much they
liked it, we entered the UK's number-one BBQ
competition, Grillstock, in Bristol. Somehow, we won
Best Burger. Off the back of that we got entered
into the World Burger Championships in Las
Vegas. We got drunk, we gambled, and somehow
managed to fend off some of the best chefs and
restaurants on earth to come second in the world.

That back-garden BBQ turned into pop-ups and
festivals, which turned into a restaurant and a food
truck, which turned into more restaurants, more
food trucks, a *Sunday Times* bestselling cookbook,
and a full-blown restaurant and events business.
Mad times.

Now, here we are with our second book. The first
one was our love letter to burgers. We poured
years of patty smashing, greasy fingers, late-night
cook-offs and burger competitions into those
pages. Burgers are what we are known for. They
are our passion and the reason The Beefy Boys is
what it is today.

But our origins are BBQ. Those early Beefy Boys
BBQs always had burgers, but they also had lamb
shoulders smoking away, steaks over hot coals, ribs,
wrapped in foil, chicken on the rotisserie, whatever
we could get our hands on, we would grill. We love
BBQ. It is how we started. BBQing became more
than just a hobby; it was a passion and a way of life.

So when it came to a second book, we knew it
had to be about BBQ. Proper BBQ. Using wood
and fire as not just the heat but as a seasoning
in its own right.

We started looking at all the BBQ books we love.
There are loads of brilliant ones. Most written by
people with far more knowledge and skill than
us. So we asked ourselves what we could bring to
the world of BBQ books that would actually add
something new.

It struck us that we couldn't think of a single cookbook that looked at BBQ through a genuinely British lens. In fact for some people the idea of British BBQ is a joke. They say it is not part of our culture like it is in other countries and that as a nation we don't live and breathe BBQ. They are wrong. It is totally part of our culture. It always has been. And judging by the explosion in UK BBQ over the last 20 years, there is clearly an appetite for it. So we set out to write a book that captures a truly British perspective on BBQ. A book that celebrates the dishes, the ingredients and the humour of the UK. Something that feels British in the best way and uses BBQ as the lens to talk about who we are today.

We have broken the book into three main chapters: Great British BBQ, Transatlantic BBQ, Multicultural BBQ.

In the first section, we want to cover BBQ that celebrates and innovates from British tradition. In the second, we reinterpret the American low-and-slow classics from the country that inspired our journey into BBQ. And in the third, we celebrate the dishes brought here by the amazing people we know whose food and culture have shaped modern Britain and helped shape The Beefy Boys as well.

We hope you enjoy this book. It has been a lot of meat, a lot of smoke, and a lot of trial and error. We hope you learn some things and cook some things and most of all we hope it makes you want to get outside and fire up your BBQ regardless of the weather.

Summers in the UK are usually temperamental. It is going to rain. So you might as well BBQ all year round; you won't notice the difference. Get outside. Get cooking. Get an umbrella. And get ready for the Great British BBQ.

First of all, what do we even mean by the word BBQ? The answer is way more complicated than you might think.

Ask an American what they mean by BBQ and they might talk about large, tough cuts of meat cooked lovingly over smouldering wood, the smoke flavouring the meat and building up layers of 'bark', the rich, dark coating that covers your briskets and pulled pork, protecting the succulent melt-in-the-mouth meat inside. This conjures images of Southern pitmasters honing their craft over years, built on a culture that stretches back through BBQ shacks, the Deep South and the Great Frontier, all the way to the Native Americans cooking over the dying embers of a fire and teaching European settlers the magical art of the barbecue.

Then if you ask an Australian what they mean by the word BBQ, they'll likely talk about grilling hot and fast, cooking steaks or shrimp over direct heat from a gas, charcoal or wood barbecue. Catching up with friends under the blistering Antipodean sun to share good times and good food, the BBQ to an Aussie is a cultural phenomenon. Gathering over a few tinnies and chargrilled meats or fish is as integral to the Australian identity as kangaroos, Mad Max or Bluey.

To Brits, traditionally the term barbecue conjures up images of paper plates, wasp attacks and the very real threat of salmonella. Picture an array of disappointing burnt or undercooked sausages and frozen burgers, a disposable BBQ bought from a petrol station, sunstroke, warm cans of beer and a fist fight over who's in command of the hi-fi stack you've moved outside using the extension cord your dad uses for the Flymo. I am being a little facetious here. That intricate picture I just painted for you was the stark reality of the British BBQs of my youth, but in the couple of decades since we have seen what can only be described as a renaissance in British BBQ. (I am using the word BBQ in this book to cover BBQ in its broadest and most watered-down terms: food cooked outside, ideally over wood, charcoal or, yes, as much as it pains me to say it, even... even gas.)

Brits have grabbed the whole concept of BBQ by its fall-off-the-bone horns. Up and down the country these days, there are countless men and women ready to bore whoever they can corner against a wall about their BBQ setup at home, spinning tales of the weekend cookout and exchanging pictures of this week's ribs like proud fathers sharing photos of their newborns. I will admit that a gaze through my phone gallery is a mixture of pictures of my kids gradually getting older, bits of meat I've cooked and the occasional spicy meme I've saved for a rainy day.

As a nation, we have become obsessed with BBQ, which is kind of mad for a country that has on average three days of sun a year, two of which tend to be in March for some reason. Yet we persist

GET
SMOK
EY

and persevere, and for those of you out there as obsessed as we are with the art of BBQing, you don't just wait for a sunny day. It's a 365-day-a-year, come-rain-or-shine way of life.

Despite all this love in the UK for BBQ, our reputation for it, especially on the world stage, is poor. British BBQ in general terms has no identity. Broadly, with some exceptions, it's fallen into the trap of just copying what other cultures and countries do and losing a lot in translation on the way. Don't get me wrong, there are some amazing chefs in the UK pushing the envelope when it comes to fire cookery, but in general British BBQ is, at its worst, a pale imitation of what they do in the States; nowhere near the glory of the original. We are the grilling equivalent of an accountant from Scunthorpe trying to struggle through the trickier parts of a Freddie Mercury vocal on *Stars in Their Eyes*.

Even those well versed in the global phenomenon of live fire cooking will concede that the UK has no real history or culture of BBQ or cooking over fire. Well, we are here to challenge that preconceived notion. I've dragged my family to many a castle ruin around the UK on a wet Sunday. I've looked past my children's and wife's bored and indifferent faces and I've seen the giant kitchens and fire pits of medieval England. Of course we have a history of cooking over fire. From the banquets of Henry VIII to the chop houses of Victorian London, our skills in roasting meat were legendary across the world. It's just that the rich history has been forgotten and lost to the ages.

We are here to take that forgotten culture and reinterpret it for the modern age so we can truly feel proud of the concept of 'The Great British BBQ'.

So, let's wind the clock back and, before we get into the cooking, have a look at the long-forgotten history of British BBQ.

WELCOME
TO Fabulous
LAS VEGAS
NEVADA
THE BEEFY
BOYS
BEEF STOCK
BEEF STOCK
BEEF STOCK
THE BEEFY
BOYS
THE BEEFY
BOYS
THE BEEFY
BOYS
THE BEEFY
BOYS

THE HISTORY OF BRITISH BBQ

So, how far back do we have to go to get to the roots of Britain's lost BBQ culture? The answer is pretty damn far. The earliest evidence of cooking over fire in the UK stretches all the way back by about 400,000 years to Beeches Pit in Suffolk, where archaeologists have found hearths containing charcoal, flint and the charred bones of animals. Kind of mad to think that almost half a million years ago a couple of cavemen had a BBQ, didn't tidy it up, and 400 millennia later some bloke in Hereford is writing about them in a book. Messy bastards.

Fast forward to the Ice Age, where you'd think firing up the barbie and having a relaxing afternoon cooking some meat was probably the last thing on a Mesolithic mind. However, lots of evidence from archaeological digs across the UK shows that open-fire cookery and grilling over flames was alive and well in the harshest of conditions. Even then you could not underestimate the tenacity of the British BBQ. One beam of sunlight is all it takes for us to fill a beer garden or fire up a grill, and it's great to see the same was true even in the Ice Age.

By the Neolithic and Bronze Age, farming communities had started to develop across the UK and large outdoor hearths, ovens and cooking pits became common. Archaeologists have found evidence of the first pieces of early BBQ equipment, including large metal cauldrons and firedogs used for supporting spits over the hearth (one of the most famous finds of the time being the Battersea Cauldron, found in 1861). The main fire cooking techniques in this period involved roasting meats with wooden or metal spits over flames, or boiling meats up in a wood-fired cauldron.

By the Iron Age, communal feasts had become a big part of society. Across seasonal festivals and tribal gatherings, evidence from Durrington Walls near Stonehenge shows that whole pigs were roasted over fire. These cook-offs were huge events in the Iron Age calendar, and the joy of meat cooked over fire was a major occasion. Early Irish literature tells tales of the champion's portion, where the choicest cut of a fire-roasted beast would be given to the bravest and strongest warrior at the feast. Often these rituals led to disputes about which warrior deserved the best cut, disputes settled in combat. This resonates even to this day. I've definitely had some steaks and BBQ in my life that I would be happy to fight a man to the death for. Albeit that man would need to be extremely weak and feeble and easily defeated by a bloke in his 40s with no training and no combat experience.

The Romans conquered Britain in the 1st century CE and, along with their funny haircuts, little skirts and complicated battle tactics, they also brought new cooking techniques to a country obsessed with stabbing each other over a slice of beef. The Romans brought the raised masonry hearth to

the UK, a fire built against a brick wall and filled with charcoal. Iron tripods and gridirons were built to support pots, pans or grills above the fire. The Romans also introduced to the UK our first domed bread ovens. They were big into feasting, and your average Roman BBQ consisted of everything from pork, beef, lamb, deer and poultry, often turned on a spit by hand. A beloved Roman BBQ snack was the dormouse. Unfortunately, this book contains no recipe for Roman dormice. If you think you are getting my family's secret dormouse kebab recipe you've got another thing coming, mate.

Around the 5th century, the Romans decided they'd had enough of our sunny weather and friendly disposition, so they packed up and went back to Rome to watch Russell Crowe fight a CGI tiger. Leaving us Brits to our own devices, our cooking practices became much simpler, revolving around a wood-fired hearth used to both heat the home and cook on. The majority of meals at the time would have been cooked in cauldrons, with grilling or roasting generally reserved for special occasions. Pork was the most popular meat in the country, with beef being reserved for the more well-to-do in society. Lamb and goat were mainly reared for wool, only hitting the dining table near the end

of their lives. The same could be said for chickens, which were generally raised for their eggs. Game cooked over fire was commonplace at feasts and celebrations. Many of these were based upon earlier Pagan traditions that were co-opted by the new Christian religion sweeping the country. Large gatherings were marked by cooking vast amounts of meat over fire. King Alfred is said to have welcomed a visiting abbot with a table 'laden with roasted meats' and a fire that burned through the night. Even in those days, Brits were getting their mates round for a BBQ.

As we move from the Anglo-Saxons to the Normans, large-scale feasting and cooking over fire became even more popular, with some castles being built with wood-fired hearths big enough to cook an entire ox. It was in the later centuries of the Norman era that Brits gained the nickname *Les Rosbifs* due to our national obsession with roasting meats. Large castles would have a member of the kitchen affectionately known as the spit boy, whose sole purpose was to keep the spits turning and the meat roasting. Larger banquets would require teams of spit boys working around the clock to keep the lords and ladies well fed with roast meats of all kinds.

Some of these recipes have survived to this day. The 14th-century cookbook *A Forme of Cury* has numerous spit-roast recipes; for example 'Cormaryer', a pork loin marinated in red wine, coriander, caraway, garlic and pepper, served with a gravy made from the drippings. It's incredible to think that 700 years ago we were using advanced techniques and spices from all over the world, especially when you consider my grandparents in the 1980s thought white pepper was adventurous and regarded spaghetti with suspicion.

As we headed towards Tudor and modern Britain there were many innovations in live fire kitchens, the main being the upgrade of the spit boy to the

highly unethical (yet cheaper) spit dog. These dogs
would be used to turn a wheel in the kitchen that,
in turn, kept the spit moving. It's unclear whether
the spit boys were happy about this, but progress
is progress, and I'd suggest if a dog can do your job
better than you, it's probably time to retrain and
seek new employment. Spit dogs are no longer
deemed acceptable, and as much fun as it would
be for us to introduce a dog into the kitchen at
work, I'm relatively sure environmental health
would have a few things to say about it.

As well as dog-based kitchen innovation, the
post-Tudor world saw open hearths being
replaced by cast-iron stoves and enclosed ranges.
Despite the move away from live fire cooking
at home, Britain was still obsessed with meat
cooked over the fire. Novelist Henry Fielding, an
18th-century observer reflecting on British cookery,
noted that 'the English love their meat plain and
roasted, over a brisk flame, basted only with its
own dripping'.

The 17th to 19th centuries saw the rise of the British
chop house. These no-fuss eateries were places
where tradesmen, clerks and professionals could
gather to drink ale and eat large cuts of meat
roasted over the fire. The chop house was no
nonsense: sawdust on the floor, big wooden tables
and minimal furnishings. The type of kitchen
fit-out that would probably cost north of a million
in a trendy BBQ spot in Soho. The traditional chop
house stayed staunchly traditional, shunning
the more fashionable French cookery from
across the Channel and sticking to traditional
meat-and-potatoes cooking. Fundamentally, the
chop house was a place where people could gather
to enjoy the finest in fire-cooked meat and real
ales. In other words, paradise.

As we moved into the modern era, our great
history of cooking over fire was lost. We became
domesticated, our kitchens became convenience-
led, and two world wars, rationing and scarcity

saw Britain's proud culinary history fade from
memory. Skills weren't passed down, recipes were
forgotten, and we lost our lust for fire. The years of
spit-roasted meats and griddle-iron cookery were
slowly replaced with gas burners, electric ovens
and, nearer the modern day, canned foods and
ready meals. I am generalizing massively here, and,
of course, we have always had a certain amount
of fantastic cookery in this country, but you would
find it hard to deny that our love for fire, and the
skills that gave us the nickname *Les Rosbifs*,
had faded.

It's only been in the last 20 years or so that we
have seen a renaissance in British fire cookery, with
everyone from high-end chefs to backyard BBQers
catching the fire-cooking bug. Our goal with this
book is to reclaim British BBQ and help connect
modern British BBQ with our rich history. Inspired
by our cousins over the pond and influenced by
the multiculturalism of modern Britain, we want
to lay the groundwork to help solidify what the
hell British BBQ is, was, and could still be.

So, you are ready to start your journey into BBQ. Now, I know some of you reading this will already be seasoned BBQers or self-proclaimed pitmasters. This section isn't for you. This is for those just starting their journey into BBQing. It can be daunting and confusing, but hopefully this section will answer some of your questions and leave you feeling less confused by the end.

Now this is probably the question you need to look at first, and there is no right or wrong answer. Picking a BBQ is a personal choice. The decision you make will affect what you will be able to cook, how you will cook, what utensils you'll need and how much effort it will require. Let's get one out of the way.

GAS BBQ

Gas BBQs are probably the most popular style in the UK, the pros being minimal fuss and minimal effort. You can be ready to cook in a few minutes, you don't need to worry about fuel or ash, it's versatile (the majority of recipes in this book will work fine on a gas BBQ unless otherwise stated), and the technology these days even allows you to achieve some form of smoking.

Is a gas BBQ right for you? For me it comes down to effort and how much you are bothered. My preference is to cook over charcoal or wood because I view the flavour you get from both to be an ingredient in and of itself, and part of the magic of cooking BBQ. Don't get me wrong, you will 100% be able to make delicious food on a gas BBQ, but it will be missing that extra bit of magic that coal or wood gives to food. The trade-off, though, is that it's far easier to use, maintain and cook on.

I cook BBQ because it's fascinating – it's never the same twice. You have to think on your feet not only about the recipe, but also the fuel source, the position of the coals, the dryness of the wood, the flavour of the smoke. A million variables all going on at once and all requiring your attention. But when you get it right you are rewarded with not only delicious food but a true sense of accomplishment.

If that sounds like a right pain in the ass and a load of stress for little return, look at gas. But make sure you have a gas BBQ with at least two burners so you can practise two-zone cooking. More on that later.

DISPOSABLE BBQS

Should be banned.

TYPES OF REAL FUEL BBQS

ASADO/CAGE BBQ

These are crazy bits of kit, making a huge visual impact and giving the chef multiple options on how to cook. They are great for direct grilling or cooking meat low and slow, using distance from the heat source instead of smoke to control temperature. They are also great for cooking multiple items at once, and it is the law in BBQ world that whenever cooking on one you must hang a pineapple from it, or some veg. The reason for this has long been lost to the BBQ gods.

BULLET BBQ

Similar to the kettle BBQ, bullet BBQs are relatively cheap in BBQ terms (which is very much like being tall in hobbit terms). Despite being designed to lean more towards smoking meats, they can still be used for direct grilling. The bullet BBQ generally has three sections: the heat source at the bottom, a water pan above it for moisture, and then the grill grates and lid at the top where your chosen meat sits. The bullet BBQ excels at smoking, and if you are after a BBQ primarily for smoking meat on a budget, then a bullet BBQ can be a great choice.

FIRE BOWLS

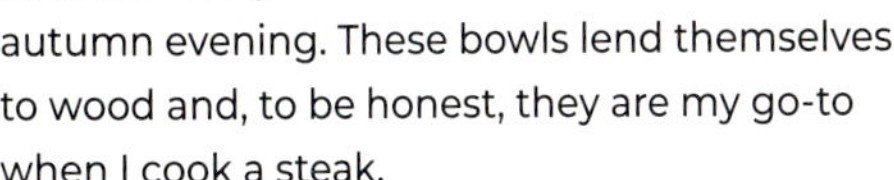

Fire bowls are basically fire pits that you can cook on. This is great because if you aren't using them for cooking, you can use them as a fire pit in the garden, which is lovely on an autumn evening. These bowls lend themselves to wood and, to be honest, they are my go-to when I cook a steak.

They also now come with myriad attachments to make them versatile. Most of these involve some mechanism to hang meat over the fire source or lean it against it, in what is known as an 'asado', a traditional Argentinian form of BBQ that takes the principle of low-and-slow cooking but achieves it by increasing the distance between the meat and the heat source. Fire bowls are great and aesthetically pleasing, as they can sit in the garden and not look like a BBQ but more like a piece of furniture. It's definitely one of my favourite ways to grill.

KAMADO

There are many brands of kamados you can look at, but they all have one thing in common: they are expensive, and with good reason. Kamados are ceramic and incredibly efficient at holding heat. This makes them great for long cooks, and while they might be expensive to buy, they are far cheaper to cook on, only requiring minimal amounts of coal to cook for long periods of time. They are also extremely versatile and are great for cooking things low and slow or hot and fast.

The ceramic walls get so hot that you can cook on them like a pizza oven, reaching temperatures of around 400°C/750°F+. The downside is you won't be able to look your partner in the eye and tell them how much it cost. You'll only be able to look at the floor and mumble quietly under your breath. Legend has it that once a leap year, between full moons, small versions appear for a radically reduced cost in that weird aisle at Lidl where you can buy everything from power tools to paddle boards. Personally, I think this is an urban myth. If you want to go kamado, start saving now.

KETTLE BBQ

One of the greatest inventions of the 20th century – up there with sliced bread, the Technics 1210 and Mario Kart. The kettle BBQ is a cost-efficient, multi-use grill, ideal for direct grilling steaks or chops or, with a bit of ingenuity, perfect for low-and-slow BBQ, from pulled pork to ribs. The kettle is a great investment and is amazing for beginners or experts. It also won't break the bank, meaning you can look your partner in the eye and actually tell them how much it cost.

The design doesn't really look like a kettle, more like a flying saucer. The bottom half contains a grate for the coals to lie on and then a grill grate above for your food to sit on. They also come with a lid, and it's this lid that makes the kettle usable as a smoker.

PELLET SMOKERS

As the name suggests, these BBQs are designed for one thing: smoking. Instead of the classic stick burner or kettle design, pellet smokers electronically smoulder pellets of flavoured wood, creating smoke. These automated smokers take the pain and effort out of regular meat smoking, allowing you to set a temperature and walk away, go to bed, or do whatever you want while the smoker maintains steady heat and smoke.

This is something unthinkable with almost every other form of smoker. Most BBQ enthusiasts, myself included, have nightmare stories of taking your eye off the BBQ for one second only to realize it's jumped 70°C and the meat you spent a fortune on, that had been lovingly smoking for hours, is now ruined. So, if you want to smoke meat but still have a social life, see family and not spend 14 hours staring at temperature gauges or fireboxes, a pellet smoker might be the best solution for you.

The trade-off is that it isn't quite as good as doing it over wood or charcoal. It's very nearly there and still delicious, but in my opinion it doesn't quite hit the spot that real wood does.

SANTA MARIA GRILL

Santa Marias are designed for direct cooking over your heat source. They come with an adjustable grill, meaning you can get close to the coals for searing or raise the grill high for gentle low-and-slow cooking. It's not enclosed, so traditional smoking won't work quite the same, but you can still get some delicious results. Santa Marias for me are the perfect steak/hot-and-fast setup. The adjustable grill height provides real drama and theatre to your BBQ while also being a great way to control temperature.

STICK BURNER/OFFSET SMOKER

These are the beasts, the massive BBQs you see pitmasters in Texas using. They generally comprise two chambers: one where you have your fire or heat source (for the bigger offsets this will be 100% wood; smaller ones may use a bed of coals to get the heat going and add wood for flavour). They are incredibly impressive and designed for one thing: low-and-slow American-style BBQ. I would never advise a stick burner or large offset as someone's first BBQ. It's a real skill and these bits of kit are for BBQ obsessives or people who want to cook huge amounts of low-and-slow BBQ in a commercial setting.

WOOD-FIRED OVEN

When we think of wood-fired ovens we inevitably think of pizza, but that's selling them short. They are fantastic for roasting, direct grilling and even, to a certain degree, smoking. I'm lucky enough to have a pizza oven at home and it's amazing how much you can do in it. Roasted veg is a game changer – the high heat of the oven cooks the veg evenly while the lick of flame from the wood provides an incredible depth of flavour.

If you purchase a Tuscan-style grill to go with your pizza oven, you can direct grill as well. A Tuscan grill sits over the embers in your oven, allowing you to cook hot and fast – everything from steaks to chicken and fish. Scrape the embers under your Tuscan grill as flames lick the roof of the oven above, cooking items quickly with direct heat from above and below. This is a fantastic way to cook and really shows off the versatility of a wood-fired oven.

BEEFY
BBQ
PIT-CREW

FUEL SOURCE

What's the difference between wood, lumpwood and briquettes?

WOOD does what it says on the tin: it's wood. It's great to use for BBQ in two ways: smoking, as in using a classic American-style offset stick burner, or as chunks thrown onto beds of coals in something like a Weber kettle or bullet smoker. Or alternatively to burn down to embers, where you are effectively making your own coals from scratch. I quite often do this if cooking on my Kadai fire bowl, Asado grill or Fire Cage.

LUMPWOOD is wood that's been burnt and starved of oxygen, creating coals. These are great for BBQ, especially when cooking hot and fast in what's known as direct grilling. Lumpwood gets to temperature quickly and, if you're sourcing decent lumpwood, it can provide fantastic flavour to food. The negatives are it can burn fast and it can be tricky to manage and maintain steady heat.

BRIQUETTES are made by taking lumpwood charcoal (or even coconuts), turning them into dust and sticking them back together with a flavourless adhesive. This might sound manufactured and not nice, but actually briquettes are a godsend, especially when doing a long cook. You can usually get a good 3–4 hours minimum of solid heat out of briquettes. Whenever I am doing something that requires a few hours, e.g. rotisserie chicken, I will opt for briquettes. If I need hot and fast heat for something direct like a kebab or steak, I will opt for lumpwood.

Please avoid any self-lighting briquettes or any fuel that has a coating to help it ignite. We are looking for clean flavours and we want nothing imparted into what you are cooking other than the flavour of the wood or charcoal itself.

There's a smorgasbord of BBQ tools, equipment and gadgets out there for you to spend the family savings on, but the only essential bits of kit you need are a grill to go over the fire, and a set of tongs. Everything after that is stuff that, while not 100 percent essential, will just help make your life easier and your BBQ better.

CAST-IRON PAN

If you're outdoors and cooking over fire, a cast-iron pan is an essential bit of kit. Shove it on the coals or straight into a pizza oven to heat up. The last thing I want when BBQing is to be running back and forth to the kitchen and taking my eye off the grill. If I'm cooking a steak and I want to make a sauce, I want to do it right by where I'm cooking the star of the show. So, get yourself a cast-iron pan; it's a fire cook's best friend.

CHIMNEY STARTER

'Game changer' is an overused phrase, generally coming from the same sort of people who also say things like 'blue sky thinking', 'OMG', 'cool beans' or 'I am here for it'. But, in the context of a charcoal chimney starter, it's worth the cringe: they are a game changer. One of the big negatives of coal-fuelled BBQ is waiting for it to be hot enough (more on that later). Chimney starters make this way more efficient and you can go from zero heat to beautiful white coals, perfect for cooking on, in as little as 15–20 minutes.

How does it work? The principle is easy. A charcoal chimney starter is a cylinder of metal with an internal grill about one-fifth of the way up. You start a fire with paper or natural firelighters in the bottom chamber, the heat rises and heats the coals evenly. Within about 15 minutes you should have some beautiful coals ready for your BBQ.

GRILL BASKETS AND GRILL TRAYS

Ever lost asparagus between the grill grates? I have. It's so upsetting. Avoid this by using a grill basket or a grill tray. These are designed for cooking things that are too small or thin to sit directly on the grates. They are hugely versatile, perfect for cooking chopped veg, fine beans or shellfish. It's an amazing way to get that smoky grill flavour onto food items that traditionally are a nightmare to grill.

GRILL BRUSH

You've got to keep that grill super clean. Not only does it look better, it also stops your food from sticking and gives you a cleaner cook. You just want the flavour of the food you're making plus the fire, you don't need the residual grease or carbon of the pork chop you cooked two weeks ago tainting your food. Try to avoid grill brushes with hard metal bristles; nobody wants to end up with a wire bristle in the mouth or, even worse, in their stomach. Ideally get yourself one where it's all one piece, and the chance of leaving anything behind on the grill after using it is minimal.

MINI FLAME THROWER

I am a busy, impatient and very disorganized man. I don't have 15 minutes to wait for my charcoal to be lit, I want instant heat. The best way to get that is with a gas-powered flame torch. These things can speed up the chimney starter process even further, giving you beautiful coals to cook on in about 5 minutes.

It's effectively a large blowtorch, but if you need to get those coals red hot real quick, it's invaluable. They're also great for allowing you to imagine yourself as Ellen Ripley torching a xenomorph egg on LV-426, while you quietly fire your coals in the back garden. The only downside is the constant fear that one of your children will get hold of it and blast their sibling, like Kurt Russell taking down a three-headed dog in the Arctic. Word of advice: keep it well out of reach of children and/or drunk BBQ guests at all times.

SPATULA

We have burgers in this book, and, due to our history as The Beefy Boys, my affinity with a spatula is so strong these days that if I was dropped on a desert island with the choice of only one thing to help me survive, it would be a phone so I could call for help. But if I was given the choice of a second thing, it would be water purification tablets. If you offered me a third choice, it would be a spatula. Great for lifting burgers off the grill, you can even slice an onion with one if you really try. You need a metal one strong enough to withstand a lot of pressure being put on it as you scrape the patties from the grill. A versatile bit of kit that I would be lost in a kitchen without.

TEMPERATURE PROBE

It's the 21st century. Get a temp probe. You are not impressing anyone by saying you can match the doneness of a cut of meat with your fingers and thumb. All cuts of meat have different textures, and the thickness of any given cut changes the way it feels when cooked. After years of practice, you do get to the point where intuition and skill mean you need your probe less, but for quality and safety purposes, get one. It will 100% make you a better cook.

These days they're relatively cheap for a good instant-read thermometer, and thanks to technology you can even get probes that stay in the meat for the entirety of your cook, connecting to your phone, notifying you when the temperature has risen or fallen and even when to take the food off the grill.

TONGS

Where would we be without tongs? A&E, that's where, as we'd be forced to handle red-hot food with our bare hands. Get yourself a good pair of BBQ tongs. I like to have more than one pair so I can avoid cross-contamination between raw and cooked food. It's also imperative, if using tongs, to clang them together a couple of times before using, just to make sure they still work.

WOOD CHIP BOX

This is for those of you using a gas grill. These little boxes work as a way to impart some smoky flavour into your food. Place different wood chips in the box and, as the grill heats up, they start to smoulder, providing light smoke flavour to your food. Is it as good as the real thing? No. But will it help add another level of flavour to your food? 100%.

Throughout this book we are cooking BBQ in multiple different ways. While certain BBQs may be more adept at certain styles, most BBQs these days can be adapted for different cooking methods. A lot of BBQ obsessives are also lucky enough to own multiple setups; if that's you: well done, don't listen to anyone else – you keep stocking up on those BBQs.

For this section we will list some of the most useful BBQ setups. One thing that makes your BBQ as versatile as possible is owning one with a lid. That simple addition to a normal grill opens up a world of possibilities.

Take all these suggestions as a rough guide. Understand the principle of what you need and work out how best to achieve that on your setup.

2-ZONE DIRECT GRILLING

This is the classic BBQ setup and the one that most people will be used to. Get a good bed of hot coals going in your BBQ. Anywhere from 30–50 percent of your BBQ should be covered with coals, leaving the other half free.

This setup gives you direct hot heat and a cool zone. Having the two zones in front of you gives you maximum control when grilling hot and fast. Getting flare-ups? Move it to the cool zone. Grill charring your meat too much? Move it to the cool zone. Want to finish your food off slowly after searing? Move it to the cool zone. If you want to slowly start rendering fat on a pork chop, lay the pork on the cool zone with the fat nearest the fire.

Two-zone direct grilling is classic BBQ as we know it in the UK, and is one of the setups you will use the most. This setup is great with lumpwood, briquettes – or a mix if you want the hot direct heat and flavour of lumpwood and the long, steady burn of briquettes.

As you progress on your BBQ journey, a more advanced version of 2-zone is gradient grilling, where instead of just stopping the heat source dead, you slowly thin the coals out to give you a range of heat across one grill; experiment, see how you get on and what works for you!

BBQ ROASTING

Roasting is the bedrock of British cooking, and doing it with charcoal or wood is a great way to take a time-honoured technique and add that extra flavour that only live fire can bring. Throughout the book, whenever we talk about BBQ roasting, this is the setup we mean.

If you are lucky enough to own one, a wood-fired pizza oven is the ultimate way to BBQ roast, but you can get results just as good on a kettle or kamado BBQ.

Set the bottom of your grill up with a small pile of briquettes or lumpwood on either side of the base, leaving a gap in the middle. You can use this gap as an extra cooking space for roasting veg, but be aware it will get hot. Alternatively, you can help lower the overall temperature of the BBQ by placing a pan of water in the middle.

Set your grill grates above the fuel source and place whatever you are roasting in the centre with the lid on. A great trick is to put your potatoes or veg in a roasting tin on the grill grates and place a second grate on top of that for your meat to sit on. The juices will fall straight into the veg as you cook.

SMOKER

Learning how to smoke food opens up a whole world of possibilities. Most smoking recipes will require you to cook from 120–135°C/250–275°F. In a small kettle or kamado, this can take a lot less fuel than you think.

For setups like that, briquettes are best to use as your primary fuel source because you will get a good 3–4 hours without reloading. You then use chunks of smoking wood or wood chips to add smoke and flavour.

When smoking you want to keep the environment nice and moist. Load between 20 and 30 percent of the base of your BBQ with briquettes. Add your smoking wood to the briquettes, then place a pan of boiling water inside.

If using a kettle BBQ, place your grill grates on top, then add a secondary water pan directly above the coals and place whatever you are smoking next to it. This gives you a moist cooking chamber and helps temper the heat.

If using a ceramic kamado, place the heat deflector directly above the coal bed, then add a water pan on top of that, followed by your grill grates. All that's left is to place your chosen meat on top and the lid. You are smoking, baby.

SPIT ROASTING AND ROTISSERIE

A hugely traditional part of classic British live fire cooking, spit roast is essentially turning meat on a spit next to a fire.

To set your BBQ up for this, place your hot coals on either side of your BBQ just as for BBQ roasting (see opposite). Place your grill grates on top and put a pan in the gap between the coals. This pan can hold water, veg, or be used simply to catch the juices and basting liquids so you can use them again during the cook.

You can do this method with the lid on or off. Using the lid speeds the process up because it turns the spit into a full rotisserie oven. Lids aren't essential, though, and rotisserie setups can work anywhere. All you need is a fuel source and a rotating spit and you are good to go.

'HOT AND FAST'

Hot and fast generally refers to the technique of cooking over direct hot heat. Searing a steak or charring vegetables, for example.

'LOW AND SLOW'

Low and slow generally refers to American-style BBQ cooking, smoking meat where the temperature is low and flavour is built up by the use of smoke.

'FLARE UPS'

Flare ups are when fat or oils from whatever you are cooking fall onto the heat source, creating flames. Sometimes a little bit of flare up can be great to add smoky flavour to your food, but it can also quickly become too much, burning your food and leaving the inside raw, or adding an acrid, charred taste to your cooking.

'THE STALL'

This is what happens when cooking a large cut of meat, like a pork shoulder, or a brisket. You are trying to cook these cuts to 93–96°C/199–205°F, and somewhere between late 60s°C/150°F and early 80s°C/176°F it will seemingly stop cooking and instead of rising in temperature it will get stuck. You will panic, you will crank up the heat, you will start thinking, 'what the hell am I going to serve?' – but don't worry, it's a natural part of the process where moisture on the outside of the meat reaches an equilibrium with the heat, causing the process of the heat moving through the meat to stall. It will pass, and you can use methods like the Texas crutch 'wrapping in foil or butcher's paper' to overcome this.

'DIRTY SMOKE AND GOOD SMOKE'

When smoking meat, conventional BBQ wisdom is that you always want nice transparent wisps to subtly flavour your meat as it cooks. That is true, but, in reality, you want to have a short spell of dirty smoke at the start of the cook to build up that bark. Dirty smoke is where the smoke is cloudy and white; you tend to get good smoke when the fire is burning well and dirty smoke when it's not quite hot enough or the airflow isn't great around the wood. Be careful, though, as too much dirty smoke can seriously ruin a good bit of BBQ.

'THE PIT'

The pit is a term sometimes used to describe a BBQ: 'Throwing the brisket on the pit' also sounds well cooler than just BBQ.

'THE COOK'

The cook is a term used to describe the long period of time taken to cook your chosen item of BBQ. You can use this when chatting to a fellow BBQ enthusiast: 'How did the cook go?'

'BARK'

Bark is the dark, rich, often black outer coating of a great bit of low-and-slow BBQ, and when done right it's like eating meat caramel – there's nothing in the world quite like the true flavour explosion.

'SMOKE RING'

The smoke ring is the red ring of truth that appears on the surface of meat properly smoked with wood. It's the result of the magic of combustion, meat and smoke that creates the chemical reactions on the meat, building up that bark.

BRINING

Brining is an essential weapon in a grill master's repertoire. It generally comes in two forms: wet brining and dry brining. These are pretty self-explanatory, and we tend to use them in two distinct ways...

DRY BRINING

Dry brining works with all meats and fish. At its most basic level it involves rubbing your chosen protein with salt, but herbs, spices and sugars can also be used.

Ideally, dry brine 24 hours before cooking, but anything from an hour onwards still helps. The salt draws moisture out of the meat, mixes with the rub, then gets pulled back into the protein through osmosis. This seasons deeply rather than just the outside.

Dry brining is hugely effective for steaks, chops and chicken. Leaving the meat uncovered in the fridge overnight also helps build a better crust or crispy skin.

WET BRINING

Wet brining involves dissolving salt, sugar and spices in water and fully submerging the meat, ideally overnight or for 24 hours. The salt and flavourings transfer to the meat and keep it moist and flavourful throughout the cook. Wet brines tend to be 8–10% salt to water, and you can also add other tenderizing agents and flavourings to your basic wet brine of just salt. This method is perfect for white meats, and for a great example try the brined chicken on page 46.

MARINATING

Marinating is when you sit meat or fish in a flavoured liquid, usually acidic or enzyme-rich. Yoghurt and pears, for example, contain natural enzymes that break down muscle fibres and tenderize meat. Great for layering flavour before you even hit the grill.

INJECTING

Injecting brines or marinades is brilliant for large cuts like pork shoulder or whole hog cooks. Cheap injection kits online will become your best friend. Injecting makes sure the inside stays moist and seasoned, not just the outside.

BASIC DRY BRINE

You will need:

1 steak (any cut, but definitely better for thicker cuts 500g/1lb 2oz and above)
SPG (salt, pepper, garlic granules; see page 33)

Method

Prep your steak, score the fat and rough up the surface with a sharp knife. Pat dry. Season liberally all over with SPG. Place on a wire rack, uncovered, in the fridge overnight.

The next day, dust off excess seasoning and get cooking. A finishing sprinkle of crunchy rock salt just before serving adds a perfect salty pop.

The basting brush is an essential part of our grilling setup. It doesn't matter if we are doing chicken, steak, pork or lamb, the basting brush is coming out. It's your tool to build up flavour and crust. It also looks super cool, but unlike most things that look cool in a kitchen, the basting brush is actually useful and serves a purpose. Basting your cut of meat with a herb brush and a basting liquor brings layers of flavour to your food. Each time you baste and sear, you are building up those layers.

MAKING A BASTING BRUSH

I like to use a wooden spoon turned upside down with butcher's string. Take a selection of herbs; the general go-to is thyme and rosemary, and that will be a solid herb brush for almost everything you cook on the grill. You can switch things up by adding other semi-woody herbs like oregano, mint or marjoram. Experiment and see what works.

Get your herbs into a large bunch, insert the bottom of the wooden spoon into the centre and wrap tightly with butcher's string. Make sure you wrap it tight; you will be battering and basting your meat with this brush, so it's got to hold together. Once you are happy with it, it's time to get your basting liquor together.

BASTING LIQUOR

Our go-to basic basting liquor is butter and garlic. From there you can take it where you like; put the butter and any other ingredient in a pot or pan and melt the butter over the heat, then keep this warm for basting throughout the cook.

A little acidity goes a long way, a squeeze of lemon or a glug of vinegar will help get those tastebuds tingling. Other herbs will work well with a butter-garlic basting liquor and so will whole chilli for a bit of heat. Think about any flavour that might complement what you are cooking, ideally avoiding anything too sugary, as sugars may burn. Try different things out, let your imagination run wild; sometimes it's the craziest ideas that work out the best. Check out our Marmite butter-basted bavette recipe on page 106.

SPIT COOKING

If we had to pick one type of BBQ that has the best claim to being a proper British take on grilling over fire, it would be cooking on the rotisserie, or spit roasting. Man has been cooking over fire, turning meat on a stick, since time immemorial all around the world, but there is something that truly speaks to the British culture, country and history about roasting a slowly turning piece of meat over a well-controlled fire.

Aussies have the barbie, the Japanese have the yakitori grill, the Yanks have the smokers; it is high time Brits claimed the title of Kings of the Spit. Even the culinary superiors over in France had to concede British prowess in cooking beef over fire, christening us *Les Rosbifs*. For those of you who failed French at school, that translates as The Roast Beefs, which is pretty damn cool. Let Americans take the title of Pitmaster. Let the British build a nation of Spitmasters.

Every time we cook on the spit we are repeating a tradition that stretches back to before the Druids who built Stonehenge, through the Romans, Saxons, Vikings, all the way to the Tudor banquets and the chop houses of Victorian London. The meat, the fire, the slow turn. And the beautiful

thing is that the principle has never changed. To quote Robert May in his 1660 book *The Accomplisht Cook*: 'Roast them plain, baste them with butter.' Which, in all honesty, also works as a way of condensing the contents of this entire book down into seven words.

Cooking meat on a spit over fire is the absolute best way of roasting meat. Do a side by side comparison, and rotisserie-cooked meat wins every time. The slow rotation allows the juices to flow around the cut as it turns, and the heat attacks the meat evenly all over. What it does to a piece of meat is magical.

Not everyone is lucky enough to own a rotisserie, but fear not. All of the recipes referring to a rotisserie can be achieved on a BBQ by roasting your meat and turning it throughout the cook. It won't be as juicy or as evenly cooked and delicious as its spit-roasted cousin, but it will still be great.

One final note: all the spit roasting recipes in this book were created on a rotisserie setup with a lid. This is not essential, but the lid does speed up the cooking process, so just be aware that if you are using a completely open rotisserie, your cook time may be longer.

HAND RULE

One of the great things about cooking over fire is that it is not a science. Well, actually, it massively is a science. What I mean is that it is not straightforward. You cannot turn the heat up by twisting a dial or pressing a button. You learn to cook over coals or fire by feel, intuition and practice.

The beauty of BBQing is in the different results you get from cooking at different temperatures and at different distances from the heat. Sometimes you want intense heat. Sometimes you want something in the middle to render fat or slowly caramelize. And sometimes you want it really low for big cuts, thick chops or just keeping something warm while you finish something else. The way we test this is the Hand Rule:

LOW HEAT

Perfect for roasting joints, really thick steaks and chops or keeping cooked food warm while you finish something else. Aim for 8–10 seconds with your hand over the heat before it gets too hot and you have to pull away.

MEDIUM HEAT

Ideal for rendering fat on chicken wings or lamb chops. A gentle heat that caramelizes slowly. Here you should be able to hold your hand for roughly 4–5 seconds.

HIGH HEAT

Great for searing steaks, chops, roasting joints or quick cooks like chicken breast or fish.

To test it, hover your hand over where the food will cook. If you can only hold your hand there for 2 seconds before pulling away, it is high heat.

DISCLAIMER

WE CAN NOT BE BLAMED FOR ANY BURNS CAUSED IN THE PROCESS OF THE HAND RULE. FIRE IS HOT. YOU CAN BURN YOURSELF. BE CAUTIOUS AND CAREFUL.

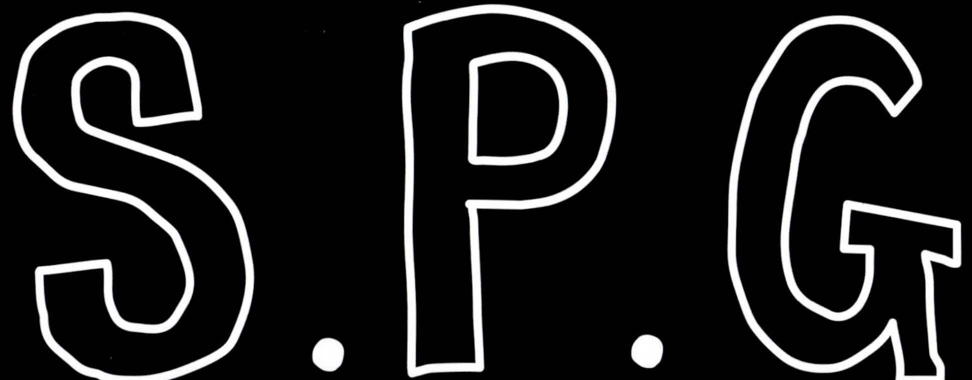

BASIC SPG

4 parts rock salt
(smoked or regular)
1 part cracked black pepper
2 parts garlic granules

Throughout this book we will refer to SPG. What is that, I hear you cry? Well, it is not the Special Patrol Group used by the Greater Metropolitan London Police Force. It is, in fact, the holy trinity of salt, pepper and garlic granules. It is the bedrock of BBQ and of cooking any meat or fish. This is your starting point. It is always great with just these three things. Beyond this it is your world to experiment.

If I am cooking pork, I will start with SPG as a base and, depending on my mood, I will throw in sage, rosemary, fennel seeds or thyme. When cooking chicken, I might add smoked paprika, chicken powder or maybe some cumin; whatever I fancy at that time.

SPG gives you a good base flavour to work with. Throughout the book we have suggestions for combinations or rubs and herbs to combine. Our favourite type of BBQ is BBQ that is not constrained, so try experimenting or keep it dead simple with SPG.

GREAT
BRI
THE BEEFY BOYS

TISH
BBQ

INGREDIENTS

Rapeseed (canola) or non-virgin olive oil, for brushing
HP gravy (see page 64)
Butter, for spreading
Salt and ground black pepper

For the fry-up

4 fat pork sausages
4 large mushrooms
2 large tomatoes, halved
Fresh (or dried) thyme
4 thick slices of bacon, ideally home-cured (see page 38)
4 rounds of black pudding, sliced 1.5cm (⅝ inch) thick
4 eggs
1 x 400g (14oz) can of baked beans
4 slices of white bread

For the breakfast potatoes

4 medium to large potatoes (Maris Piper or red), cubed
2 tbsp beef dripping
½ tbsp salt
¾ tsp dried sage
¼ tsp dried rosemary
¼ tsp dried thyme
½ tsp garlic granules
¼ tsp ground black pepper

Here's how to cook a **Full English on the BBQ** with a few live-fire twists and a banging HP gravy.

Smoke the sausages. Set your BBQ up for smoking and get it running steady at 120°C/250°F. Place the sausages on the smoker with a chunk of apple wood and smoke for 25–30 minutes until they hit 65°C/149°F internal temperature. Remove and set aside.

Grill setup. Switch your BBQ to a 2-zone direct grilling setup. Brush your mushrooms and tomatoes with oil, season with salt, pepper and thyme, and place them over direct heat. Sear for 2–3 minutes per side, then move them to the cooler zone to finish slowly.

Make the HP gravy. Follow the instructions on page 64.

Make the breakfast potatoes. Par-boil the cubed potatoes in salted water until tender, then drain and cool. Melt the dripping in a frying pan over a medium heat. Once fully melted add the potatoes. Fry for 5 minutes, stirring, then add all the herbs and seasonings. Continue to fry until golden and crispy on the outside and puffy in the middle.

Fry the bacon, sausages and black pudding. Place a cast-iron pan on the BBQ. Slowly fry off your bacon until crisp on both sides, then add the smoked sausages to the same pan. Keep turning until the sausages are golden and reading 75°C/167°F internal temperature.

Grill the black pudding directly over the coals, turning every minute until it hits 75°C/167°F.

Prepare the eggs, beans and bread. Crack your eggs straight into the cast-iron pan. Warm your beans in a pan on the grill. Toast your bread Texas-style over the coals until golden, and butter them up.

Assemble. Plate up your sausages up with all the bits, then pour the gravy into a jug (pitcher) and stick it in the middle of the table.

HOME-CURED SMOKED BACON

BBQ setup: Offset smoker, kettle, kamado or bullet smoker

Fuel source: Briquettes are best for a long smoke like this, or all wood in an offset

Wood flavour: Fruit woods like apple or cherry work brilliantly. For a stronger smoke flavour, go with oak, hickory or mesquite

Cook time: 3–4 hours, plus 4 days curing

INGREDIENTS

1kg (2lb 4oz) pork belly (rind removed)

50g (1¾oz) smoked salt

50g (¼ cup) brown sugar

25g (1 tbsp plus 1 tsp) maple syrup

Bacon is a British institution. It's what keeps the country ticking over. The problem is, a lot of bacon you buy these days is rubbish. You start cooking it and white foam seeps out of the sides. The best way to guarantee you're eating amazing bacon? Make it yourself.

In the UK we're famous for our love of back (loin) bacon, but for this home-cured and smoked version, I'm going with belly. Don't judge me – the shape is even, it's affordable, and it's easy to get hold of. That makes it the ideal cut if you want to try curing your own.

This recipe uses no nitrates. Just salt, sugar and smoke to cure and flavour. It won't keep as long as nitrate-cured bacon (you'll get 3–4 days in the fridge once smoked), but the trade-off is worth it. This will probably be the best bacon you've ever eaten.

Place the pork belly in a large zip-lock bag. Add the salt, sugar and maple syrup. Seal the bag and massage everything in, making sure the meat is well coated.

Lay the bag flat in the fridge for 3 days. Turn the pork once a day in the morning and once in the evening before going to bed, giving it another quick rub as you do so, to move the brine around.

After day 3, remove the belly from the bag. Let any excess brine drip off. Place the pork on a wire rack over a tray and leave it uncovered in the fridge overnight to dry out.

Set your BBQ for smoking at around 120°C/250°F. Add your chosen wood and get a nice clean smoke rolling. Place the pork belly on the grill and smoke until it reaches an internal temperature of 93°C/200°F.

Remove from the smoker and let it cool. Place in the fridge and once it's fully chilled, it's ready to use.

To cook, slice thickly, from 1–2cm (½–¾ inches), and fry in a pan until caramelized.

This bacon also works brilliantly chopped into cubes and fried off like pancetta. It will freeze happily to extend its life, or keep it in the fridge for 3–4 days.

Serves: 6–8

BBQ setup: Rotisserie

Fuel source: Lumpwood and/or briquettes

Cook time: 6–7 hours, plus optional 24-hour dry brining

INGREDIENTS

3–5kg (6½–11lb) piece of pork belly, skin on, boned, skin scored

Salt and ground black pepper or SPG (salt, pepper, garlic granules; see page 33)

Optional chopped fresh or dried herbs: thyme and/or rosemary, sage, fennel seeds

Smoked rock salt

For the stuffing

1 onion, diced

1 tbsp pork or beef dripping

1 tsp salt

3 garlic cloves, diced

2 tbsp dried sage

1 tbsp dried parsley

1 tsp garlic granules

1 tbsp onion granules

½ tsp cracked black pepper

400g (14oz) panko breadcrumbs

500ml (2 cups) chicken stock

TOP TIP

To make a hog roast roll: chop up the pork stuffing and crackling, whack it in a bun with our smoked apple butter (page 214).

Rolled pork belly, or Italian-style porchetta, is the best and easiest way to get a hog roast experience, without cooking a whole pig! Here, we use a classic butcher's hog roast stuffing, it's not as fancy as our stuffing on page 72; feel free to swap it out if you're feeling posh.

For the stuffing, fry the onion in the pork or beef fat with the salt to help it soften. After about 5 minutes, add the garlic and dried herbs. Cook for another 10–15 minutes to caramelize the onions, then add the garlic granules, onion granules, black pepper and the panko. Stir well so the breadcrumbs absorb the flavour. Pour in the chicken stock and stir. The breadcrumbs should drink up all the liquid. Remove from the heat and cool completely in the fridge.

Lay out the pork belly, meat side up. Season all over with SPG and any extra herbs. Add the stuffing, pushing it into every nook and cranny. Roll the pork up tightly and secure at intervals with butcher's string.

To prep the skin, place a rack in the bottom of your sink with the plug removed. Slowly pour a full kettle of boiling water over the skin. You will see it tighten and change colour instantly. This helps blistering later. Pat the skin dry. Crush some smoked rock salt to a fine powder and rub it liberally all over the skin. Place the pork on a rack in the fridge, uncovered, overnight to dry the skin out fully.

When ready to cook, set your BBQ up for rotisserie cooking. Load the spit with the pork and place it on the BBQ with the coals pushed to the edges and a tray underneath to catch drippings. Add your briquettes, lumpwood, or a mix, and put the lid on.

Your BBQ will start around 200°C/400°F but will naturally settle around 150°C/300°F. Try to maintain it there. Check the internal temperature throughout; you are looking for around 93°C/200°F. At this point (after 5–6 hours) the pork should be fall-apart tender with crispy crackling.

If the crackling has not fully puffed, move the coal baskets directly underneath the pork or as close to the skin as possible. You may need to switch the rotisserie off and let the skin sit next to the heat, but watch it like a hawk. For stubborn patches, grab a red-hot coal with your tongs and hold it near the skin to finish the job.

Serves: 6–8 (depending on size)

BBQ setup: BBQ roasting

Fuel source: Lumpwood, briquettes, or wood burnt down to embers

Cook time: 7–8 hours, plus optional overnight dry brining

INGREDIENTS

1 whole shoulder of lamb

3 garlic cloves, cut into slivers

A couple of sprigs of rosemary

Salt and ground black pepper or SPG (salt, pepper, garlic granules; see page 33)

Spritz made of ⅓ red wine vinegar and ⅔ water

Pickled red cabbage, to serve

For the potatoes

2kg (4lb 8oz) King Edward or other floury potatoes

Butter, for greasing

1 tbsp thyme (fresh or dried)

2 onions, thinly sliced

1 litre (generous 4 cups) chicken stock

Huge amount of inspiration here from a British favourite, Lancashire Hotpot, but with a live fire twist by cooking the lamb shoulder whole and sitting it above the potatoes so all that beautiful lamb fat coats the spuds, making them crispy, rich and packed full of flavour.

Prep the lamb. Ideally do this the day before. Using a sharp knife, make tiny little 1cm (½ inch) slits all over the lamb. Take a sliver of garlic and one tiny sprig of rosemary and push a pair of each into each slit. Season the lamb all over with salt and pepper (or SPG). If prepping the night before, leave it uncovered in the fridge overnight to dry out the skin and dry-brine the lamb.

Prep the potatoes. Peel the potatoes and slice them thinly (no more than 5mm/¼ inch) – a food processor works well for this.

Grease the inside of a cast-iron pan with butter. Layer the potatoes in the pan, adding thyme, a light seasoning of salt and ground black pepper and onions between every few layers. Pour over the stock.

Roast the lamb and potatoes. Set your BBQ up for BBQ roasting and place the potatoes in the centre. Position a wire rack directly over the potato pan and place the lamb shoulder on the rack.

Cover with the lid and roast for about 2 hours at around 180–200°C/ 350–400°F. After that, you can let the temperature drift down to around 120°C/250°F for a final couple of hours, to keep the lamb juicy.

Check the lamb every 30–45 minutes; spritz each time with the vinegar mix. If the skin is getting too much colour, loosely cover with foil.

The lamb is ready when it hits 93–94°C/199–201°F internal temperature. As soon as it's there, take it off the heat and let it rest for 20–30 minutes.

The potatoes should now be golden, but if they need more colour you can leave them in the BBQ and get the heat up while the lamb rests.

Serve. Pull the lamb apart using a pair of spoons and serve it up with those dripping potatoes and pickled red cabbage.

Serves: 6–8

BBQ setup: Rotisserie

Fuel source: Lumpwood or briquettes

Cook time: 2–3 hours, plus optional overnight dry brining

INGREDIENTS

1 rolled sirloin of beef (2–3kg/4lb 8oz–6lb 8oz)

About 2 tsp English mustard

Salt and ground black pepper or SPG (salt, pepper, garlic granules; see page 33)

Basting liquor (melted butter and beef fat, rosemary, thyme and garlic; see page 28)

Legend has it that the sirloin got its name after a king took a bite of beef that was so good he whipped out his sword and knighted it on the spot. Kind of mad that an inanimate piece of meat can gain the highest honour known in the land when there are far more deserving recipients out there, like people who win burger competitions. But we digress.

A well-cooked piece of sirloin slowly roasted over the fire this way will be one of the best pieces of beef you've ever put in your mouth. One bite and you'll fully understand why this joint of beef received a knighthood.

Prep your sirloin the night before. It should already be rolled, but because of the way heat transfers through meat, it's wise to ask your butcher to tie it as tightly as possible so it's nice and round. If it's a bit square, you can press it gently into shape on the counter.

Grab the mustard and rub it all over your beef, then season heavily with salt and pepper (or SPG). Ideally, leave it uncovered in the fridge overnight.

Set your BBQ up for a rotisserie with coals on either side. You want hot heat at the start of this cook. In a regular kettle BBQ, split a whole chimney starter of briquettes (with a little lumpwood) between both sides. Place a tray directly underneath the beef to catch the drippings.

Mount your beef on the spit and roast it over a high heat for 30–45 minutes. If your rotisserie has a lid, put it on now. Check every 15 minutes and baste each time, using a mix of your basting liquor and the drippings from the pan.

Once you've got the colour and crust you want, slow things down. You can do this by removing the lid or simply letting the fuel burn down naturally without topping it up. This slow, long finish will make the beef beautifully tender and perfectly pink from edge to edge.

Remove the beef when it hits around 52°C/125°F. Let it rest for 15–20 minutes, then carve it up and serve.

Serves: 4–6

BBQ setup: Rotisserie

Fuel source: Lumpwood or briquettes

Wood flavour: Optional mild wood like apple or cherry if you want a touch of smoke

Cook time: 1 hour 30 minutes, plus 24-hour brining

INGREDIENTS

1 chicken (1.6–2kg/ 3lb 8oz–2lb 4oz)

Oil, for coating the chicken

Handful of thyme and rosemary leaves

Par-boiled potatoes tossed in beef dripping or duck fat

2–3 tbsp melted butter

Cracked black pepper and a light sprinkle of extra salt if needed (but be careful, the brine seasons heavily)

For the wet brine

1.5 litres (6 cups) water

150g (5½oz) smoked salt

50g (¼ cup) sugar

100g (3½oz) bicarbonate of soda (baking soda)

120ml (½ cup) cider vinegar

10 garlic cloves, peeled

A few sprigs of rosemary

A few sprigs of thyme

3 tbsp fennel seeds

1 tbsp black peppercorns

3 bay leaves

Bicarb chicken is wild. It takes the Chinese velveting technique and applies it to a whole bird. The bicarbonate of soda (baking soda) makes the meat more alkaline, which stops the protein fibres tightening up during cooking, meaning you get one of the most tender and juicy roast chickens you will ever eat. (If you don't have a rotisserie, try setting up your BBQ for BBQ roasting and turning the chicken over halfway through the cook.)

Add all the brine ingredients to a large pan and bring to the boil until everything dissolves. Allow the brine to cool completely, then refrigerate until stone cold.

Submerge the whole chicken in the cold brine and leave refrigerated for 24 hours.

Remove the chicken from the brine and pat dry thoroughly. Oil the chicken lightly and season with cracked black pepper, thyme and rosemary. Add extra salt only if needed.

Set up the BBQ for rotisserie cooking with hot coals on either side and a drip tray underneath. Place your par-boiled potatoes in the tray, tossed in beef dripping or duck fat.

Mount the chicken on the spit and secure tightly. Roast at around 200°C/400°F with the lid on, basting with melted butter every 20 minutes.

Remove the chicken when the breast reaches the high 60°Cs/ mid-150s°F and the thighs and legs read above 75°C/167°F internal temperature. If any skin areas need crisping, a quick blast with a blowtorch will sort it right out.

Rest the chicken somewhere warm and uncovered for 20 minutes.

During the rest, top up the coals and crisp up your roast potatoes on the BBQ with the lid on.

Carve up your ridiculously juicy chicken, serve with your crispy roasties and at least 3 gallons of gravy.

Serves: 4–8

BBQ setup: Smoker

Fuel source: Lumpwood, briquettes, or all wood in an offset

Wood flavour: Oak, hickory, cherry

Cook time: 6–8 hours

INGREDIENTS

1.5kg (3lb 5oz) whole beef chuck

SPG (salt, pepper, garlic granules; see page 33) or your favourite BBQ rub, or salt and coarsely ground black pepper

2 onions, halved and sliced into half-moons

3 garlic cloves, finely diced

1 tbsp beef dripping

1 tsp thyme (fresh or dried)

½ tsp rosemary (fresh or dried)

1 litre (generous 4 cups) beef stock

1 tsp Bovril

3 tbsp Worcestershire sauce

When it comes to pulled meats, pork reigns supreme. But there's something so satisfying, comforting and rich about a fork (or fist) full of pulled beef.

Chuck is economical – one of the cheaper cuts of beef – but it also lends itself brilliantly to smoking and braising because of its fat content. This is a great 'do it the day before' recipe: cook it, pull it, leave it overnight in the fridge in a pan with its cooking liquor, then reheat the next day. Perfect if you've got mates round and you don't want to be glued to the BBQ all day.

I like to split a piece of chuck of this size, so you get maximum bark – more bark means more flavour! Split the chuck into 2–4 pieces and season all over. Get your smoker running at 120–135°C/250–275°F with some nice rolling smoke, and place your beef on the grill. Smoke for 3–4 hours until a good bark has built up.

While the beef's smoking, sweat off the onions and garlic in a large pan with the beef dripping, thyme and rosemary. Keep the onions over a low heat so they soften slowly and caramelize.

Once the beef's had its 3–4 hours and you're happy with the bark, take it off the smoker and chop the chuck up into large chunks. Place the chunks in the pan with the onions and garlic, then pour over the beef stock, Bovril and Worcestershire sauce.

Now you can either return the pot to the smoker with the lid on to slowly braise, cook it gently on the stovetop, or pop it in the oven at 120°C/250°F with the lid on.

The beef should take another 3 hours or so, or until it's tender enough to fall apart and pull. Once ready, break up all the meat, stir it through the gravy and serve.

Serves: 4–6

BBQ setup: BBQ roasting

Fuel source: Lumpwood
or briquettes

Cook time: 1 hour 30 minutes,
plus 24-hour brining

**1kg (2lb 4oz) pulled and braised
beef chuck (see page 48), plus
its cooking liquor**

**1 tbsp beef fat (skimmed from
the smoked chuck, or regular
beef dripping)**

1 tbsp plain (all-purpose) flour

150g (5½oz) Cheddar, grated

For the mash

10 large potatoes

2 marrow bones, split

130g (generous ½ cup) butter

240ml (1 cup) milk

Salt and ground black pepper

**This recipe is also a great way to use smoked and braised
chuck. And the bone marrow mash will change the way you
make mash forever.**

Set up your BBQ for roasting, and prepare the beef according to
the method on page 48.

Melt the beef fat in a pan. Add the flour and mix to form a roux.
Start ladling in some of the cooking liquor from the braised beef.
We want to build a rich, deep gravy.

Slowly add more of the braising liquor until you have a thick, well-
bodied gravy. Add your pulled meat and stir it through. Taste and
adjust the seasoning. You may need to add a little beef stock. The
goal is a rich meat-and-gravy filling with a proper balance of both.
Pour the meat and gravy into a baking dish or tray and set aside.

To make the mash, bake the potatoes in a hot oven or on the BBQ
until tender enough to easily put a knife through. Roast the bone
marrow over the coals with a light seasoning of salt and pepper.
Once softened and cooked through, set aside.

Halve the potatoes and press them through a sieve (strainer) while
holding the potato skins in your hand to protect you from the heat.
Once all the potato is sieved, add the bone marrow and butter. Stir
through the potatoes, then slowly pour in the milk, stirring all the
time. Season and set aside.

Once the mash has cooled slightly, spoon it gently over the meat
mixture. Take one of the marrow bones and stand it upright in
the middle of the dish or tray so the pie bakes with a dramatic
centrepiece bone chimney.

Sprinkle the grated Cheddar over the mash and BBQ roast for around
40 minutes until the top is golden and the whole pie is piping hot.

Boom: ready-to-go BBQ cottage pie!

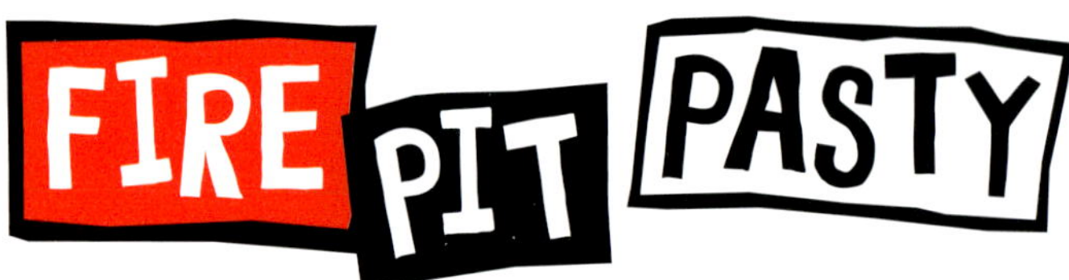

Serves: 6

BBQ setup: BBQ roasting

Fuel source: Lumpwood, briquettes, or wood burnt down to embers

Cook time: 1 hour, plus 3 hours resting the pastry (plus cooking the beef)

INGREDIENTS

1kg (2lb 4oz) pulled and braised beef chuck (see page 48), chilled

400g (14oz) Cheddar (or smoked cheese), grated

250g (9oz) pickled jalapeños, or to taste

For the shortcrust pastry

460g (3½ cups) plain (all-purpose) flour, plus extra for dusting

1 tsp salt

150g (⅔ cup) cold salted butter

150g (⅔ cup) very cold beef dripping

600ml (2½ cups) ice-cold water

To finish

1 egg, beaten

Rock salt

Pasties hold a special place in the hearts of the British. Originating in medieval times and popularized by Cornish miners, the concept of meat and pastry with a crimped edge to keep your fingers clean has inspired everything from its own tax to multi-gazillion-pound high-street giant Greggs.

It's the miners of Cornwall we need to thank. Mining was an industry that helped build this country and propelled us through the Industrial Revolution. We should never forget how hard life was for the miners.

To help my kids visualize what life was like as a miner, I locked them in a dark room and forced them to play Minecraft while eating a pasty. Occasionally I would come in dressed as Margaret Thatcher and tell them to turn it all off. Until I realized that this is basically what they do every day anyway. (Apart from the me-dressing-up-as-Margaret-Thatcher bit – that's reserved for my OnlyFans.)

Anyway, this is a pitmaster's pasty. Beef, cheese and jalapeño are always a winning combination, and everything is better when wrapped in delicious shortcrust pastry.

To make the pastry, add the flour and salt to a bowl and stir to combine. Add the cold butter and beef dripping (the colder the better). Work the fat into the flour using your fingertips, until the mixture looks and feels like coarse breadcrumbs. (You can also do this by pulsing in a food processor.)

Slowly add the cold water, mixing as you go, until it comes together into a dough. Be careful not to overwork the dough or it will make the pastry tough rather than flaky. Once combined, wrap the dough in cling film (plastic wrap) and place it in the fridge for a minimum of 3 hours, or up to 3 days.

Set your BBQ up for BBQ roasting.

Take the dough out of the fridge and lightly dust your surface with flour. Divide the dough into 6 equal balls. Roll each ball out, then use a plate as a guide to cut a large circle.

Layer the beef filling onto one half of the pastry, followed by the cheese and as much jalapeño as you fancy. Wet the edge of the pastry, fold it over and seal. Crimp the edge using your fingers to pinch and fold. It is also acceptable to get frustrated and just fold it over and press it with a fork – just don't tell your Cornish uncle. He will cry.

Brush the pasties with the beaten egg and sprinkle with a little rock salt.

Get your BBQ roasting at 170°C/340°F. Place the pasties on a baking tray and cook in the BBQ for 45–50 minutes, or until golden and cooked through. Let them cool for 10–20 minutes before tucking in.

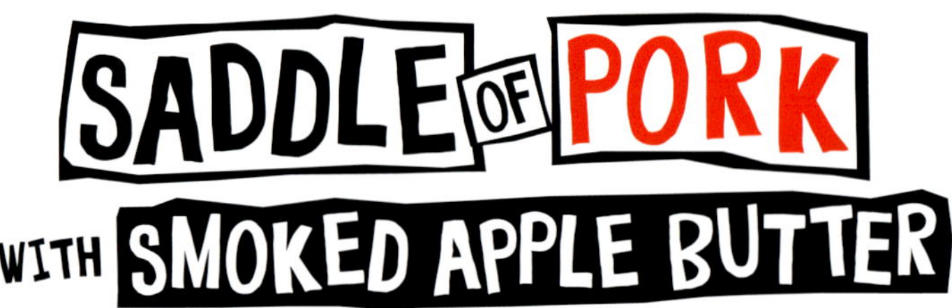

Serves: 6–8 (depending on size)

BBQ setup: 2-zone direct grilling, BBQ roasting and smoker (for the apple sauce)

Fuel source: Lumpwood, briquettes, or wood burnt down to embers

Wood flavour: Oak (smoking apple with apple feels weird)

Cook time: 2½–3½ hours, plus overnight dry brining

INGREDIENTS

1.5–3kg (3lb 5oz–6lb 8oz) bone-on, French-trimmed pork saddle, skin scored (the bigger the joint, the longer the cook)

2–3 tbsp fine salt

3–4 tbsp pork rub (see page 74)

Smoked apple butter (see page 214)

TOP TIP

Taste the smoked apple butter: depending on your apples, you might want to add a bit of sugar for sweetness or cider vinegar for balance.

I always feel like pork is the forgotten roast dinner. Beef's the showstopper, chicken's the everyday hero, lamb's for special occasions – and poor old pork gets forgotten about, but a bone-in saddle of pork can be a true work of art.

Prep the pork. The night before, boil a full kettle of water. Hold your pork saddle over the sink and slowly pour the boiling water over the skin, being careful not to touch the flesh. You'll see the skin react immediately – that's what we want; it shocks and tightens the skin, helping to form perfect crackling later.

Pat the skin completely dry. Rub the skin with the fine salt and the flesh with the pork rub. Place it back in the fridge, uncovered, overnight to dry-brine and dehydrate the skin.

Make the smoked apple butter. Follow the instructions on page 214 and see top tip below.

The sear. Set your BBQ for direct grilling. Take the pork out of the fridge and brush off any excess salt. Oil the grill grates, then carefully place the pork, skin-side down, over the coals.

Be vigilant here – we're trying to crisp the skin, not cremate it. Move it around as needed, flipping between direct and indirect zones until you've built a good layer of golden crackling.

The roast. Once the skin looks perfect, switch to a BBQ roasting setup at around 120°C/250°F. Slowly roast the pork until it hits 63–64°C/145–147°F internal temperature (about 1½–3 hours, depending on size).

Remove from the heat and rest. Carryover cooking will take it into the mid to high 60s/152°F which will still leave a gentle blush in the centre. If you prefer it cooked all the way through, pull the pork at around 73°C/163°F instead.

Serve. Slice the saddle into thick cuts and serve with the smoked apple butter.

Serves: 2
BBQ setup: 2-zone direct grilling
Fuel source: Lumpwood, briquettes, or wood burnt down to embers
Cook time: Under 30 minutes

INGREDIENTS

2 romaine or large baby gem lettuces
1 tbsp rapeseed (canola) oil, plus extra for the lettuce
3 garlic cloves, finely diced
650g (1lb 7oz) large, raw shelled prawns (jumbo shrimp), plus 2–4 shell-on
Juice of 1 lemon
1 tsp smoked paprika
Salt and ground black pepper

For the Marie Rose sauce
225g (1 cup) mayonnaise
120ml (½ cup) tomato ketchup
3 tbsp Worcestershire sauce
½ tsp cayenne pepper
2 tsp freshly grated horseradish, plus extra to serve
½ tsp salt
A few dashes of your favourite hot sauce

It is a little known fact that during the 1980s Margaret Thatcher made it law that all restaurants in the UK could only serve three types of starter: garlic mushrooms on toast, pâté on toast, or prawn cocktail. Luckily that law was overturned by the great soup riots of 1989, but despite this we all still love the nostalgia that a good prawn cocktail can bring.

We are switching this prawn cocktail up by grilling the prawns and the lettuce, bringing an extra level to this classic.

Make the Marie Rose sauce ideally the day before by combining all the ingredients in a bowl, stirring thoroughly, and storing in the fridge.

Get your BBQ ready for direct grilling.

Slice your lettuces in half, drizzle the cut side with oil and sprinkle with a little salt and pepper. Get them onto the grill directly over the heat for about 5 minutes to char, then remove and cool completely.

Mix the garlic with all the prawns, the oil, lemon juice, smoked paprika and plenty of salt and pepper. Place a grill basket over the direct heat and toss the prawns in the basket until they have all changed colour and are a beautiful pink, and the shell-on prawns have gone golden red.

Separate the leaves of the grilled lettuce, keeping aside 2 big ones for presentation. Chop the remaining lettuce. Load 2 cocktail glasses with the chopped lettuce and the big slice standing up, then add the grilled shelled prawns to the chopped lettuce. Add the Marie Rose sauce and top with as much grated horseradish as you dare. Place the shell-on prawns on the edge of the glass.

Get ready to party like it's 1989.

 for maximum prawn cocktail excellence.

One: when you are eating it, take the head off the shell-on prawns and squeeze their heads over the other prawns and dressing. To the uninitiated this may sound gross, but trust me, all the best flavour of the prawn is in there. It is what makes a bisque so good. Do not waste it.

Two: this is something we picked up in a great steak restaurant in Indianapolis that was recommended to us by the legendary DJ BBQ, St. Elmo's, one of the oldest steak houses in America. They are famous for topping their shrimp cocktail with an obscene amount of fresh horseradish, which makes eating it feel like a bizarre pain challenge but is somehow still delicious and gets everyone talking at the table. Mainly saying 'pass the water.' If you do not want to destroy all the pain receptors in your nasal passage, just put a bit of fresh horseradish on. If you want to feel like you can smell sounds, then load it up.

Serves: 4

BBQ setup: Direct grilling for the fish, BBQ roasting for the chips

Fuel source: Lumpwood, briquettes, or wood burnt down to embers

Cook time: 45 minutes (ideally boil the potatoes earlier in the day)

INGREDIENTS

1.5–2kg (3lb 5oz–4lb 8oz) Maris Piper or King Edward potatoes

Char tartare sauce (see page 214)

150g (⅔ cup) beef dripping

4 skin-on cod fillets, each 150–200g (5½–7oz)

Rapeseed (canola) oil, for rubbing into the fish

Salt and ground black pepper

Malt vinegar, to serve pepper

Grilled lemon, to serve

How do you do fish and chips on the BBQ without running the risk of a trip to A&E? The answer is here and involves direct grilling the fish to get that super-crispy skin, and par-boiling then BBQ roasting your chips. Combine that with the char tartare sauce and you have an amazing fish supper that tastes just like a chippy tea.

Prep the chips. Cut the potatoes into fat, chunky chip shapes.

Wash off the starch, then drop the potatoes into a pan of heavily salted cold water. Slowly bring to the boil and simmer until you can just poke a knife through them.

Drain, then lay the potatoes on a rack over a baking tray so air can get all around them. This helps dry them out.

Make the char tartare sauce. Follow the instructions on page 214.

Cook the chips. Set your BBQ up for BBQ roasting at around 200°C/400°F. Place a large roasting tin on the grill and add the beef dripping. Close the lid to get it ripping hot.

Add the potatoes and roast for 25–30 minutes, turning regularly, until golden brown and crispy.

Cook the fish. Pat the fish dry, especially the skin. Rub the fillets with oil. Heavily season the skin side with salt and pepper, going lighter on the flesh side.

Oil the grill grates really well. Once the grill hits the 2-second hand rule (see page 32), place the fish skin-side down and leave it alone. Crispy skin only happens if you let it sit. About 70 percent of the cooking time should be skin-side down. After 4–5 minutes, the edges should start to firm up. If the skin still sticks when you try to flip it, give it another minute.

Gently flip and cook the flesh side for another 2–3 minutes. Serve with the chips, vinegar and the char tartare sauce. Garnish with a wedge of grilled lemon.

THE BEEFY BOYS

Serves: 2 (as a light lunch)
BBQ setup: 2-zone direct grilling
Fuel source: Lumpwood, briquettes, or wood burnt down to embers
Cook time: 15 minutes, plus optional overnight dry brining

INGREDIENTS

450–500g (1lb–1lb 2oz) venison haunch, cut into 2.5–3cm (1–1¼ inch) cubes
1 herb basting brush (see page 28)
Basting liquor (melted butter, garlic, rosemary and thyme; see page 28)

For the cocoa rub

1 tsp unsweetened cocoa powder
1 tbsp smoked salt
1½ tsp ground black pepper
1 tsp garlic granules

To serve

Horseradish cream (see page 62)
Beetroot ketchup (see page 153)

BBQing in the UK is historically reserved for the three days of the year when it's hot. Which is daft because cooking meat over fire is one of the cosiest autumnal or winter-warming things you can do. And what could be more autumnal than venison, beetroot and horseradish? Forget a spiced latte or paying twenty quid to pick a pumpkin that was bought at a supermarket and dumped in a field. As soon as the leaves turn brown I'm thinking about what woodland creature I can get onto the BBQ, and this is one of the easiest and quickest game recipes to knock up.

Make your cocoa rub by combining all the ingredients. Toss your cubed venison in the rub, ideally the night before (leaving it in the fridge). Use thick, flat skewers to hold the meat in place for turning, and add the venison to the skewers.

Set your BBQ up for 2-zone direct grilling and get the grill to the 2-second hand rule (see page 32). Oil up the grates and place your venison skewers on the grill.

Let them sear for 1–2 minutes, turn them and baste with the liquor. Continue this process until the cubes are browned all over. Move them to the cooler part of the grill and probe the temperature. You are looking for around 52–55°C/125–131°F. Remove, rest for a minute and serve with the horseradish cream and beetroot ketchup.

Serves: 6–8

BBQ setup: Rotisserie

Fuel source: Lumpwood and briquettes

Cook time: 2½–3 hours, plus optional overnight dry brining

INGREDIENTS

1 x 3- or 4-bone rib of beef, French trimmed and tied

Worcestershire sauce

SPG (salt, pepper, garlic granules; see page 33)

1 herb basting brush (see page 28)

Basting liquor (melted butter and garlic; see page 28)

For the horseradish cream

3 tbsp freshly grated horseradish

1 tbsp sour cream

3 tbsp double (heavy) cream

1 tbsp cider vinegar

I would also argue that beef on the rotisserie over fire is the absolute best way to cook roast beef. The flavour, the caramelization and the completely even cooking makes it a winner all round. We serve this with freshly made horseradish cream. I love the stuff out of a jar, but just like everything, making it properly from scratch is the best way to go.

Douse the beef rib generously with Worcestershire sauce and season heavily with SPG, ideally the night before you cook it.

Get your BBQ set up for rotisserie cooking, ideally with a 60/40 split of briquettes to good-quality lumpwood.

Place a drip tray in the centre of the BBQ between the 2 coal zones and load the beef onto the spit. Close the lid. The BBQ should rise to around 200°C/400°F. Allow the beef to roast, turning on the spit for 30 minutes.

Lift the lid and use the herb brush to baste generously with garlic butter. Close the lid again and cook for another 30 minutes before checking the internal temperature; it should be between 20 and 30°C/68 and 86°F.

If you are happy with the colour, continue the rest of the roast with the lid off. If you want more colour, keep going with the lid on. Just make sure you leave time to finish the cook slowly. You want the internal temperature to rise gently from around 40°C/104°F to 54°C/129°F, so use a mix of lid on and lid off to guide the beef where it needs to be. Do not rush it.

As soon as the beef hits 54°C/129°F, take it off the BBQ and rest somewhere warm for 20 minutes.

While the beef is cooking, place the grated horseradish in a bowl and add the sour cream, double cream and vinegar. Mix well, season to taste and set aside in the fridge for at least an hour before serving.

Carve the beef English style (super thinly) or American style (super thick). Both approaches are correct and glorious.

Serves: Really depends on who's hogging the gravy boat

BBQ setup: Direct grilling and BBQ roasting

Fuel source: Lumpwood, briquettes, or wood if using an asado setup

Cook time: 6–8 hours, plus optional overnight dry brining

INGREDIENTS

1 beef marrow bone, split
2 tbsp plain (all-purpose) flour
750ml (3 cups) good-quality beef stock
120ml (½ cup) red wine
4 tbsp dark soy sauce
3 tbsp Worcestershire sauce
1 tbsp Bovril
Salt and ground black pepper

BONE MARROW GRAVY

As a nation, we love gravy. We eat it, we drink it, we debate it. Thick or thin? Too thick and it's like a cow pat on your roast. Too thin and it brings flashbacks of school, with thrifty dinner ladies making ten gallons of 'gravy' from just four granules of Bisto.

We sit on the gravy fence. A great gravy is neither too thin nor too thick. It should be thick enough to coat your roasties, but thin enough to fall through the prongs of a fork. This is a great gravy to serve alongside roast beef, or even sausage and mash. BBQ roasting the bones gives you that faint whisper of BBQ smoke to elevate your gravy game.

Season your marrow bone halves with salt and pepper. Place them on a BBQ set up for BBQ roasting at around 180°C/350°F and roast for about 15 minutes, or until the marrow is cooked through.

Scoop the marrow out of the bones and place it in a pan over a medium heat with the flour. Stir together to make a roux. Slowly ladle in the stock, stirring constantly so it stays smooth.

Once all the stock is incorporated, add the wine and bring it up to a simmer. Let it bubble away until the alcohol cooks off, then add the soy sauce, Worcestershire sauce and Bovril.

Check the seasoning and thickness. If it's too thin, let it bubble a bit longer to reduce. If it's too thick, add a little more stock, or water.

Serve piping hot and prepare to argue about whether it's too thick or too thin.

INGREDIENTS

2 onions, sliced
1 tbsp plain (all-purpose) flour
400ml (generous 1½ cups) beef stock
1 tbsp Worcestershire sauce
1 tbsp HP sauce
1 tbsp Bovril
1 tsp dark soy sauce

HP GRAVY

Melt 1 tablespoon of butter with a splash of oil in a pan over a medium-low heat. Add the sliced onions and cook for 15–20 minutes until soft, golden and caramelized. Stir in the flour and cook for a few minutes to form a roux. Gradually add the beef stock, while stirring, to make a smooth gravy. Once combined, add the rest of the ingredients. Stir well, taste, and adjust the seasoning with salt and pepper to taste.

Serves: Up to 8

BBQ setup: 2-zone direct grilling

Fuel source: Lumpwood or wood burnt down to embers

Cook time: 1–1½ hours, plus rendering fat

INGREDIENTS

For the lamb

1 leg of lamb (about 2kg/4lb 8oz)

Leaves from 4 sprigs of rosemary

4 garlic cloves, peeled

Zest and juice of 1 lemon

80ml (⅓ cup) oil

1½ tbsp salt

½ tbsp ground black pepper

Lamb trimmings or offcuts (ask your butcher; or use lard), for rendering fat

1 herb basting brush (see page 28)

Basting liquor (melted butter, plenty of mint, garlic and lemon juice; see page 28)

For the grilled veg

10 spring onions (scallions)

A little rapeseed (canola) or olive (non-virgin) oil

4 large red (bell) peppers

For the salsa verde

25g (1oz) parsley

30g (1oz) chopped mint

2 garlic cloves

9 anchovy fillets in oil

This dish is perfect for any lamb sceptics out there. And by that I don't mean people who don't think sheep exist, I mean people who don't like lamb. We're lucky in the UK to have some of the best lamb in the world. The grilled veg in this can be swapped around depending on the season or whatever you fancy.

Prep the lamb. Butterfly the lamb so it's as flat and even in thickness as possible (or get your butcher to do this). Use a sharp knife to slice into the thicker parts, cutting halfway through and folding them out flat; the whole leg should be about 5cm (2 inches) thick. Make your herby rub. In a pestle and mortar or food processor, combine the rosemary, garlic, lemon zest and juice, oil, salt and pepper until it forms an oily paste.

Rub the herby paste all over the butterflied lamb, getting it into every nook and cranny. You can do this just before cooking, but if you've got time, leave it overnight in the fridge for maximum flavour.

Render the lamb fat. Place the lamb trimmings on an oven tray and cook in the oven at 150°C/300°F/Gas 2 for around 30 minutes, or until the fat has fully rendered out. Strain off the liquid fat from the trimmings and keep for the flatbreads and frying later.

Grill the lamb. Set up your BBQ for 2-zone grilling. You're looking for a medium heat – you should be able to hold your hand about 4 seconds above the grill before it gets too hot. Place the lamb skin-side down over the direct heat to start caramelizing the fat. Be vigilant – if the flames rise, flip the lamb or move it to the cooler zone.

Flip the lamb every few minutes, moving it between direct and indirect heat and basting with your brush and liquor to build up a crust. The finished lamb wants to still be pink inside; we are aiming for about 58°C/136°F internal temp for medium. If you like it more well done, take it higher. Control the heat with the 2-zone setup, or by raising the grill bars if your BBQ allows. The whole process should take 60–90 minutes. Once cooked to your liking, remove from the heat and let rest somewhere warm for 10–15 minutes before slicing.

Recipe and ingredients continue...

14 OZ

1 tbsp honey
1 tbsp capers
Zest and juice of 1 lemon
1 tbsp red wine vinegar

For the flatbreads
4 tbsp rendered lamb fat (see page 66), plus extra for frying
500g (4 cups) plain (all-purpose) flour
300ml (1¼ cups) water
2 tsp salt

Grill the veg. While the lamb is resting, toss your spring onions in oil and salt, then grill them directly over the heat until charred and tender.

Place the peppers directly on the hot coals. Turn every few minutes until the skins are blackened all over. Remove from the heat, peel off the blackened skin, discard the cores and slice the flesh into strips.

Make the salsa verde. Add all the ingredients to a food processor (or pestle and mortar if you're feeling like a caveman) and blitz until you get a vibrant green sauce.

Cook the flatbreads. If your lamb fat has solidified, gently reheat it until melted. Combine all the flatbread ingredients in a bowl and mix until a smooth dough forms. Divide into 8 even balls, cover and set aside.

Place a cast-iron pan or hotplate over the coals and add a spoon of lamb fat. Roll each dough ball out flat and cook in the pan for about 2 minutes on each side until puffed and golden. Repeat with the rest.

Serve. Slice the lamb against the grain and layer it up on the flatbreads with the grilled peppers, spring onions and a generous spoonful of salsa verde. Grab a drink, get messy and enjoy – this is a proper live fire feast.

Serves: 3–4
BBQ setup: 2-zone direct grilling
Fuel source: Lumpwood, briquettes, or wood burnt down to embers
Cook time: 1 hour

INGREDIENTS

1 pork tenderloin
Herefordian white sauce
(see page 214)
1 tsp thyme leaves
1 tbsp rapeseed (canola) or
non-virgin olive oil, for the grill
500g (1lb 2oz) tenderstem
broccoli
Coarse rock salt

For the brine
2 tsp fennel seeds
2 tsp cracked black pepper
240ml (1 cup) apple juice
25g (1oz) smoked salt
110g (⅓ cup) black treacle
(molasses)
960ml (4 cups) water

Think of tenderloin as fillet steak but with pork. It's one lean, big muscle with zero fat, so it's an easy one to overcook and is definitely best served medium, still blushing. The black treacle brine works wonders on this cut, imparting a beautiful salty sweetness to the pork. The white sauce used here is our take on the classic American BBQ white sauce, and it goes great with poultry, fish, or veg as well as pork.

Make the brine. Toast the fennel seeds in a hot pan for about 45 seconds. Once aromatic, add all the other ingredients, bring to the boil so the sugars and salt dissolve, then chill completely.

Prep the pork. Trim any silver skin and any little bits hanging off so the tenderloin is neat and, for want of a better term, looks like a smooth meat cannon (grow up). Once the brine is cold, add the pork and refrigerate overnight, ideally 24 hours.

Make the sauce. While the BBQ is coming up to temperature, mix all your ingredients for the Herefordian white sauce in a bowl (see page 214).

Cook the pork. Once your grill is ready, take the pork out of the brine and pat it dry. It shouldn't need much more seasoning, but a light sprinkle of cracked black pepper and some scant thyme leaves will make it look pretty. Oil your grill grates and get the tenderloin on directly over the coals. Let it sit still for 1–1½ minutes before turning. Once you've got a good sear on all sides, move the pork to the cooler zone, close enough to pick up a nice bit of ambient heat. Probe regularly: as soon as it hits 62–63°C/143–145°F, pull it off! The carryover cooking will finish it off as it rests.

Cook the broccoli. While the pork is resting for 5–10 minutes, toss the raw broccoli in a few tablespoons of the Herefordian white sauce. This is really going to pep up that broccoli! Get it straight over the hot coals, flipping every couple of minutes until it's beautifully charred and tender.

Assemble. Slice the tenderloin into medallions 1.5–2cm (⅝–¾ inch) thick and sprinkle with a tiny bit of coarse salt. Serve with the charred broccoli and a good dollop of Herefordian white sauce on the side.

BLACK TREACLE

INGREDIENTS

1 chicken, about 2kg (4lb 8oz)

1 large onion, peeled

For the chicken rub

1½ tbsp smoked salt

½ tbsp ground black pepper

½ tbsp onion granules

½ tbsp garlic granules

½ tbsp dried rosemary

½ tbsp dried thyme

For the chicken stuffing

100g (3½oz) smoked
bacon lardons

2 medium onions, diced

2 garlic cloves, finely chopped

3 tsp dried sage

1 tsp thyme

1 tsp rosemary

1 apple, peeled, cored and diced
(or swap for other fresh or
dried fruit)

3 tbsp chopped nuts (chestnuts,
pistachios, hazelnuts –
whatever you fancy)

180g (6¼oz) breadcrumbs

800g (1lb 12oz) sausage meat

1 tsp salt

1 tsp ground black pepper

For the baste

50g (3½ tbsp) beef dripping

100g (scant ½ cup) butter

2 tbsp rapeseed (canola) oil

1 herb basting brush
(see page 28)

The slow rotation of this bastes the meat from the inside out, the butter baste builds layer upon layer of flavour, and the flavour you get from the charcoal gives it that Sunday roast existential crisis moment. You'll genuinely question every roast you've ever eaten before. This is a great base stuffing – feel free to swap the apple out or add other fruits and nuts to suit your taste. So, what are you waiting for? Start redefining the Sunday roast now.

Prep the chicken. Ideally, prep the chicken the day before. Mix your rub ingredients and season the bird generously inside and out with it. Ideally, place uncovered in the fridge overnight for a dry brine.

Make the stuffing. In a medium-hot pan, cook the bacon lardons until caramelized and the fat has rendered, about 5 minutes. Add the diced onions and cook until translucent, then add the garlic and herbs, and stir for another 5 minutes.

Stir the diced apple and chopped nuts into the pan, along with the breadcrumbs. Mix well so the crumbs soak up all that lovely onion and bacon flavour. Set aside to cool. Once cooled, mix it all together with the sausage meat, salt and pepper. Fry a tiny patty of the stuffing to test the seasoning.

Stuff the cavity of the chicken, packing it in well. Place the peeled onion inside the cavity to seal the stuffing and stop it falling out during cooking. If you have leftover stuffing, roll it into balls and BBQ roast them in a separate tin.

Set up the BBQ. Set up your BBQ for rotisserie cooking with hot coals on either side and the rotisserie running through the centre. Place your grill grates over the coals and a roasting tray in the middle underneath – this will catch the drippings and hold your baste.

Add the beef dripping, butter and oil for the baste to the tray to melt together as the BBQ heats.

Mount the chicken. Secure your chicken on the rotisserie rod. Cross the legs and tuck them under the fork attachment to lock in the onion and stuffing. Make sure it's firmly in place. Put the bird on the BBQ, put the lid on, and aim for a temperature of around 220°C/430°F.

Baste the chicken every 20 minutes all over using your herb brush. Keep the lid on between bastes to trap the heat.

Once the chicken has developed a deep golden colour, remove the lid and let it finish over a gentle heat. Check the internal temperature – you're aiming for 65–70°C/149–158°F in the breast and 75°C/167°F in the thighs.

If the skin needs a little extra crisping, remove the drip tray and move the coals directly underneath the bird. Keep basting, but be ready for flare-ups.

Rest and serve. Once the chicken is beautifully roasted and at temperature, remove it from the rotisserie and rest it uncovered for 15–20 minutes before carving.

TOP TIP

Take your basting tray, scrape out any burnt bits and use the remaining butter, dripping and chicken juices to make the best gravy of your life. Just whisk in a tablespoon of flour and a good pint of chicken stock, simmer until thick and pour over everything in sight. Or, alternatively, par-boil your potatoes and throw them in the basting liquor so they roast under the chicken as well.

Serves: 6–8

BBQ setup: Asado cross over a fire pit (or see intro)

Fuel source: Wood: apple, oak, or birch all work brilliantly

Cook time: 6 hours, plus overnight dry brining

INGREDIENTS

2.5–3kg (5lb 8oz–6lb 8oz) piece of pork belly, rind on, bones removed, skin scored (ask your butcher to do this)

120g (4oz/½ cup) fine sea salt

Spritz made of 240ml (1 cup) water and 120ml (½ cup) cider vinegar or apple juice

For the pork rub

3 tbsp smoked salt

1 tbsp garlic granules

1 tbsp onion granules

1 tbsp dried rosemary

1 tbsp dried thyme

1 tbsp fennel seeds

1 tbsp black peppercorns

This is the recipe and method for an asado-style pork belly, but if you don't have an asado cross you can still replicate the principle by getting as much distance as possible between your heat source and the meat. I'm not going to sit here and come up with an elaborate system of winches and pulleys for you to hang a pork belly over your backyard BBQ – I'll let you get creative with that one! Just remember, distance is the key.

For the pork rub, put all the ingredients in a pestle and mortar and smash it all up.

The night before cooking you need to prep your pork belly. Boil a kettle. This isn't only to have a cup a tea, it's also an essential step on your quest for perfect crackling. Hold the pork belly over the sink with tongs, and slowly pour the boiling water over the skin. Be careful not to let the water hit the meat – we're not cooking it, we're just shocking the skin to help it crisp up later.

Once the skin has been scalded, cover the meat side generously with your pork rub. Season the skin liberally with the fine salt. Don't worry, it won't end up too salty – the excess will fall away. The salt's main job is to not only add flavour but also draw moisture out of the skin. Place the pork belly on a wire rack over a tray and refrigerate, uncovered, overnight to dry out.

On the day of the cook, get a fire going with your chosen wood. While the fire's catching, set up your asado cross (or improvised alternative, see recipe intro). Attach your pork belly securely using hooks and wire. Every asado setup is different, but the key is to make sure the belly is properly fixed and won't fall off mid-cook. Also make sure the crackling side is facing away from the pole of the asado – it needs to be completely open to the fire with no obstructions to get full coverage on that all-important crackling.

When you're confident your pork isn't going to end up on the floor, it's time to get it over the fire. The best advice here is to take it slow and steady – gentle heat is the key. Hold your hand high above the fire to find the spot where you can hold it there for about 8 seconds before it gets too hot. That's your perfect pork belly zone.

Recipe continues…

Adjust your asado so the pork sits nicely in that 8-second heat zone (see page 32).

Start with the meat side facing the fire and the crackling facing away. Your job for the next 2–3 hours is to keep the fire steady and even. Add a fresh log every 45 minutes or so. I like to add logs to either side of the main fire so they warm up slowly and catch gradually – you don't want big flames licking your belly. Think steady heat with a little smoke, not a raging inferno.

Keep an eye on the pork as it cooks. Move wood or embers around if one area is getting too much or too little heat. Every 30 minutes or so, lift the belly up for an inspection. Check for any burnt spots and give the meat side a light spritz (never spritz the skin – we want that to stay dry).

After about 2½–3 hours, you should have a lovely caramelized colour on the meat side. Probe the belly; you're aiming for around 70°C/158°F. Don't worry if it's a little higher or lower – colour and texture matter more than the exact number at this stage.

Once you're happy with the colour, flip the pork so the crackling faces the fire. Keep it in that 8-second heat zone. Watch closely – you don't want the crackling to burn. Cook the crackling side for another 2–2½ hours. Start probing again. Pork belly is hard to overcook, and I like mine fully rendered at 93–96°C/200–205°F, but if you prefer more bite and fat, take it off in the mid-80s/185°F.

Once you have your pork at the desired temperature, it's time for the magic moment – the crackling. Make sure your fire is raging hot and evenly spread. Lower the asado so the pork belly is much closer to the heat. You want it so hot you can only hold your hand there for about 2 seconds. Watch the pork like a hawk. The fat will start to bubble, then suddenly the crackling will begin to bloom. Hold your nerve. Don't panic. You want that skin to puff up and go beautifully crisp without burning. As soon as it starts to colour too much, lift it away from the heat.

If there are patches that haven't quite crisped, grab a pair of tongs and hold a red-hot coal close to those areas for a minute or two. You'll see the crackling bloom right before your eyes. Once the whole skin is golden and crisp, let the pork belly rest for about 20 minutes before carving into one of the best bites of pork you'll ever have: crunchy, juicy, smoky.

Serves: 4–6

BBQ setup: Hot roasting setup (wood-fired oven is ideal, or get your kettle BBQ running hot for roasting)

Fuel source: Briquettes, or wood if using a wood-fired oven

Cook time: 45 minutes, plus overnight resting

INGREDIENTS

2 tbsp beef dripping, plus extra for greasing

475ml (2 cups) warm water

2 tsp dried yeast

2 tsp smoked salt (regular salt works fine too)

560g (4 cups) strong white bread flour (look for at least 12% protein)

Sprig of rosemary, leaves stripped

Flaky sea salt

This is a great low-effort loaf that's a real doddle to whip up and works as an awesome side with loads of dishes in this book. I mean, what's not to like – it's beef fat and bread?!

Some cynical people out there might say this is just focaccia where we've swapped the olive oil for beef dripping. To them I say… shhh.

Heat the beef dripping until just melted. In a mixing bowl, mix it with the warm water, yeast and smoked salt. Let it stand for about 10 minutes to wake the yeast up.

Stir in the flour and mix until everything is combined into a sticky dough. Cover the bowl with a damp cloth and leave for 30 minutes.

Wet your hands with warm water. Grab one 'corner' of the dough (it'll be round, but imagine corners), lift it up and fold it back over the dough. Do this with all four 'corners'. Cover and leave for 30 minutes, then repeat. You want to do this fold-and-rest procedure 4 times in total.

After the fourth fold, place the dough (covered) in the fridge overnight.

A few hours before baking, take the dough out of the fridge. Grease a deep 21 x 30cm (8 x 12 inch) baking tin (pan) with beef fat, then tip the dough into it. Use your fingers to press dimples all over the top. Leave somewhere warm for 2 hours to rise.

Heat your oven or BBQ to 230°C/445°F. Melt a little more beef dripping and drizzle it over the risen dough. Sprinkle generously with rosemary and flaked sea salt and bake for 25–30 minutes, until the top and bottom are golden and crispy.

Remove from the oven or BBQ and cool on a wire rack.

We don't eat enough game in the UK. We've got a huge abundance of it and it's delicious. The Game Tray is our way of showcasing what's out there. This isn't so much a collection of recipes as a set of ideas to get your creative mind going.

While you *can* get game in supermarkets and good butchers, some bits are harder to find unless you know someone with a shotgun and a Barbour jacket. So take the following pages as a guide – grab yourself some incredible British game and cook up a feast.

Serves: 4–6
BBQ setup: 2-zone direct grilling, smoker, spit cooking
Fuel source: Lumpwood, briquettes, or wood burnt down to embers
Wood flavour (if smoking): Apple or cherry
Cook time: A lot of game cooks quickly but the boar takes ages

PARTRIDGE, QUAIL OR GROUSE

INGREDIENTS

2 small game birds
Sage and garlic butter (see recipe right)

Set the BBQ to 2-zone grilling, coals ripping hot (2-second hand rule, see page 32). Season the birds all over, then cook skin-side down for the first 3 minutes, and turn every minute after. Baste regularly with sage and garlic butter, cooking them for 70 percent of the time on the underside.

Tilt the birds to cook the legs directly on the grill, then move to a cooler zone until the breasts hit 65°C/149°F and the legs hit 75°C/167°F internal temperature. Rest for 5 minutes.

BUTTER-BASTED PHEASANT

INGREDIENTS

A brace of pheasants (that's 2 pheasants for you townies)
SPG (salt, pepper, garlic granules; see page 33)
1 herb basting brush (see page 28)

For the sage and garlic basting butter
2 garlic cloves, crushed
200g (generous ¾ cup) butter, softened
1½ tbsp sage leaves, finely chopped

Mix the garlic with the butter and sage and rub the butter under and over the pheasant skin. Season heavily with SPG. Cook on the rotisserie, basting every 5 minutes using the herb brush. Remove when the breasts read 65°C/149°F.

VENISON AND PIGEON

INGREDIENTS

6 venison sausages
6 venison cutlets
6 skinless pigeon breasts
Melted garlic butter

Smoke the venison sausages at 120°C/250°F over oak or apple for 45–60 minutes. Remove when they hit 75°C/167°F internal temperature.

For venison cutlets and pigeon breasts, set a hot searing zone and oil the grill. Brush the meat with melted garlic butter as it cooks, turning it often. Remove both pigeon and venison at 55°C/131°F internal temperature.

WILD BOAR

INGREDIENTS

1 wild boar shoulder, 2.5–3kg (5½–6½lb)
2 bottles dry cider

For the wild boar rub

1½ tbsp salt
½ tbsp fennel seeds
½ tbsp coarsely ground black pepper
4 garlic cloves, peeled
4 sprigs of rosemary
60ml (¼ cup) oil

Smash all the ingredients for the rub in a pestle and mortar. Rub all over the boar and marinate for a few hours, or ideally overnight in the fridge. Smoke at 120°C/250°F over apple wood for 3 hours. Transfer to a large pot and add the cider to cover. Place the lid on and cook on the BBQ or in the oven at 120°C/250°F for 3–4 hours, until the boar hits 93°C/200°F internal temperature.

Rest until it cools to around 65°C/149°F, then pull the meat and toss through the cider juices.

PICKLED MUSHROOMS

INGREDIENTS

120ml (½ cup) white vinegar
360ml (1½ cups) water
1½ tbsp salt
1½ tbsp sugar
300g (10½oz) mushrooms, sliced
1 tsp thyme leaves
2 garlic cloves, peeled

In a pan, heat the vinegar, water, salt and sugar until dissolved. Allow to cool slightly. Add the mushrooms, thyme and garlic to a jar and pour over the pickling liquor.

Cool, seal and refrigerate. The mushrooms are ready in 1 hour, but better overnight.

PICKLED PEARS

INGREDIENTS

3 pears, peeled, cored and thinly sliced
2 garlic cloves, peeled
½ tbsp fennel seeds
120ml (½ cup) white vinegar
360ml (1½ cups) water
1½ tbsp salt
1½ tbsp sugar

Place the sliced pears and garlic a clean jar. Toast the fennel seeds in a small pan, then add the vinegar, water, salt and sugar. Bring to the boil, then cool for a minute before pouring over the pears.

Seal and refrigerate. The pears are ready in 1 hour, but better overnight.

BUTTERFLIED CHICKEN DRUMSTICKS

Serves: 3–4 (as a snack)

BBQ setup: 2-zone direct grilling

Fuel source: Lumpwood, briquettes, or wood burnt down to embers

Cook time: 20 minutes, plus optional dry brining

INGREDIENTS

8–10 chicken drumsticks

For the quick cupboard rub

1 tbsp salt

1 tsp chicken powder

1 tbsp garlic granules

½ tbsp smoked paprika

½ tbsp ground black pepper

For dipping (optional)

**Herefordian white sauce
(see page 214)**

Super quick, super fun, and a great little snack. If you've got the mates round for a few beers, this is an absolute winner – simple, delicious and ridiculously versatile. Any rub will work here, but I've given you a quick store-cupboard rub you can knock up in seconds.

Like all meat, these benefit from a dry brine the night before, but you can also just chuck them straight on the grill if you're in a rush.

First, prep your chicken. Using a sharp knife, slice down each drumstick, stopping just before the joint where the foot would be. Use your knife to cut slightly behind the bone, making it easier to butterfly out the meat so it kind of looks like Batman spreading his wings (well, it does to me anyway). Be careful not to fully detach the meat from the bone.

Season with your chosen rub and dry brine uncovered in the fridge, overnight or a few hours before, or just before grilling.

Get your grill red hot – follow the 2-second hand rule (see page 32). Place the drumsticks skin-side down and crisp that skin up, moving the butterflied legs every minute or so. After 3–4 minutes, flip the chicken and cook the flesh side.

Keep an eye on that skin – you want it crispy. Move the drumsticks around to target any areas that need extra colour. Once you're happy with the look of the chicken, move them over to the indirect side and finish cooking slowly, probing every few minutes until they hit 75°C/167°F internal temperature.

Take them off the grill and serve hot, either just as they are, or with a good dollop of Herefordian white sauce for dipping.

Serves: 2–4

BBQ setup: 2-zone direct grilling

Fuel source: Lumpwood, briquettes, or wood burnt down to embers

Cook time: 40 minutes, plus optional overnight dry brining

INGREDIENTS

1 rack of French-trimmed lamb

Salt and ground black pepper or SPG (salt, pepper, garlic granules; see page 33)

For the Shrewsbury sauce

1 tbsp butter

1 tbsp plain (all-purpose) flour

250ml (1 cup) chicken stock

250ml (1 cup) beef stock

60ml (¼ cup) red wine

1 tbsp dark soy sauce

1 tbsp Worcestershire sauce

1 tsp Dijon mustard

1 tsp redcurrant jelly

A rack of lamb is the most dainty of centrepieces for a roast, and when you take the time to really render the fat out you end up with a slice of meat that combines beautifully tender meat and deliciously rich fat.

Shrewsbury sauce is a traditional sauce for lamb and Shrewsbury holds a special place in our hearts as it was the location of our second restaurant. We love the town, the people and the sense of humour. We can even look past the Hereford and Shrewsbury football rivalry to celebrate the good people of Salop and their local sauce.

Prep the lamb the day before by seasoning it all over with salt and pepper or SPG.

Set your BBQ up for indirect grilling. You want to render out as much fat as possible from the lamb, so place the lamb skin-side down over a low heat, using the 8-second hand rule (see page 32). Leave it there to cook slowly, checking regularly to make sure the fat does not caramelize too quickly or start to burn.

While the lamb is rendering, make the sauce. Melt the butter with the flour in a pan over a low heat and stir until a roux forms. Slowly add the chicken and beef stocks, stirring continuously until the sauce is smooth.

Increase the heat and add the wine. Let it bubble so the alcohol cooks off, then after a few minutes add the soy sauce, Worcestershire sauce, mustard and redcurrant jelly. Check the seasoning and keep the sauce warm.

Once you are happy you have rendered enough of the lamb fat cap, it is time to sear the meat side. Move the lamb to the hot zone, where you can only hold your hand for 2 seconds, and sear the meat, being careful to protect the fat cap from burning.

When the lamb hits around 58°C/136°F, take it off the heat and let it rest for 5–10 minutes.

Slice into chops and serve with the Shrewsbury sauce.

Serves: 8–10, with leftovers

BBQ setup: Smoker, kettle, kamado, or bullet BBQ

Wood flavour: Fruit woods like apple or cherry work brilliantly. For a stronger smoke flavour, go with oak, hickory or mesquite

Fuel source: Briquettes are best for a long smoke like this, or all wood in an offset

Cook time: 5–6 hours

INGREDIENTS

1 x 2.5kg (5lb 8oz) cured gammon ham

Glaze of your choice (see page 217)

TOP TIP

If you're using a deboned gammon, keep the netting or string on tight until you come to glaze it. This helps the gammon hold its shape.

The great thing about smoking your own ham is that it sets you up for loads of other dishes: ham and parsley sauce; ham and bubble and squeak; the classic ham, egg and chips. Obviously there are ham sandwiches, but this beast will keep for a week. Slice it, fry it, cube it and chuck it into a carbonara; get some potatoes, onions, stock and ham, and baby you got yourself a stew going! Whatever you fancy. You'll get a solid 7 days of good eating out of it.

This recipe works just as well with bigger or smaller hams, just adjust your cooking times. The main thing is that you hit the right internal temperature at the end. I find the size suggested here a great size for 8–10 people with plenty of leftovers.

Set up your BBQ. Get it rolling at a steady 120°C/250°F. Add a chunk of wood for smoke.

Start smoking. Place your gammon on the BBQ with a tray of boiling water underneath. This will catch drippings and add moisture to the cook. Close the lid and leave for 4 hours.

Check the temperature. At around the 4-hour mark, lift the lid and probe the gammon. You're aiming for 55°C/131°F internal temperature. If it's not there yet, keep cooking.

Prep for glazing. Once at temperature, remove the gammon. Cut away the netting or string, then remove the rind. Score a criss-cross into the fat using a sharp knife. If you like cloves, stud them in here. Personally, I avoid them.

Glaze and finish. Place the gammon back on the BBQ and baste with your glaze every 15 minutes. Cook until the ham hits 62–63°C/143–145°F internal temperature. Take it off the smoker – the carryover heat will finish it. To be safe, your gammon needs to stay over 65°C/149°F for 10 minutes, which should happen naturally as it rests, but do your temp check to make sure!

Serve or store. Carve it hot, or let it cool and keep in the fridge for up to a week.

BANGERS

TOP TIPS FROM SOSIJ

You could not write a book about British BBQs without looking at the humble banger, often the only highlight of the average Great British BBQ of yesteryear. We love sausages so much in the UK we have them for breakfast, we have them for dinner, we roll them up in pastry so we can have them on the go, we batter them, we fry them, we wrap them in bacon so we can have them alongside a 3-stone turkey at Christmas. we even shove them in baked bean cans so we can eat miniature sausages in our beans that we have alongside our larger sausage.

We like sausage. And there is no one better to talk sausage than our good friend Alasdair from Sosij. Alasdair is a chef with over 15 years' experience. This man makes some of the best sausages in the world and he is here to share a tiny bit of his knowledge with some top tips for making your own bangers at home.

CRAFT SAUSAGE MAKING

A truly great sausage relies on just three things:

- Meat
- Fat
- Salt

That is it. Those are the bones of the whole process. Everything else is flair, personality and the occasional moment of creative madness.

MEAT VS FAT

You need to keep an open mind about fat. Fat is good. Fat is flavour. For great sausage consistency you want anywhere between 20 and 30 percent fat to lean meat.

SALT

Salt is the next most important part. For a craft sausage, anywhere from 1.7 to 1.9 percent works best.

The reason these numbers matter is that sausage making is, at its core, about ratios. People love to get whimsical with ingredients, sprinkle a handful of this and that in, and then wonder why their sausage feels like a damp disappointment. A sausage is essentially a carefully structured combination of meat, fat, salt and whatever joyful nonsense you choose to add. Get the balance right and the world is wonderful. Get it wrong and the dogs will not even look at it.

SPG: THE HOLY TRINITY

Nearly all of Alasdair's sausages begin with one dependable foundation: SPG (salt, pepper, garlic granules; see page 33 for ratios).

In BBQ circles this is not just seasoning, it is practically a religion. As long as your sausage has this trifecta it will always have a baseline of flavour you can trust. Think of it like tuning a musical instrument. Get it right and the rest of the melody can take shape.

Once that foundation is set, then the real fun begins.

FLAVOURS

Alasdair's philosophy is simple. Add ingredients into the sausage and do not overcomplicate the meat itself unless the flavour profile calls for it.

The meat is the binder, the canvas, the structural component that holds everything together. It should be good quality, of course, but it does not need to act as the star of the show. The excitement comes from the flavours you build inside:

- Aromatic flavours
- Cheese
- Herbs and spices
- Textural surprises
- Components that make the eater raise an eyebrow and say, 'well that is rather good'

The joy of craft sausage making is creating little edible worlds inside a skin. You are not just making a sausage, you are building a bite.

LESS IS MORE

The temptation is always to chuck in more spices, a mountain of paprika or a heroic spoon of cumin, and hope for the best.

Resist it. Subtlety is where craftsmanship lives.

Use spices sparingly to shift the flavour profile, not dominate it. If garlic is your engine, spices are your steering wheel.

Do not be afraid of textures either. A sausage should be fun to eat. A surprise of sweetness, a crunch, a whisper of heat. These are the things that separate a proper sausage maker from someone who is merely having a go.

THE NON NEGOTIABLES

Honestly, you do not need a laboratory. You just need the right basics.

Grinder: For achieving a consistent mince without turning everything into grey paste.

Sausage stuffer: Do not, I repeat do not, attempt to stuff sausages with a grinder attachment. That path leads only to misery.

A spare fridge: The greatest discovery of sausage makers everywhere. You need somewhere to hang, chill and rest your sausages without the rest of the household shouting at you.

OTHER BITS AND BOBS

- Sausage skins (ask your butcher)
- Sturdy trays for mixing and piping
- Cocktail sticks for dealing with trapped air
- Blue J-cloths because sausage making is not tidy and you will soon accept that

IN SUMMARY

Craft sausage making is equal parts precision and play. Respect the ratios, honour your SPG, use good pork and good fat, and then let your imagination loose within reason. A sausage should be expressive, delicious and ever-so-slightly mischievous.

And if in doubt, add more garlic.

Let's face facts: steaks are expensive. Our advice is eat less steak throughout the year, but when you do eat steak go all out, get the best meat you can and treat that steak with the love and respect it deserves. Cooking a steak for us is about having the time to really enjoy the process. This section is about listing all the techniques you can use to take your steak to the next level. You don't need to use all these techniques and, in all honesty, we don't do every single one every time we cook a steak, but each listed will add that extra little something to layer up flavour and give you (hopefully) the best steak you've ever had.

PICKING YOUR STEAK

DRY AGING

When picking a steak, dry aging is one of the first things we look for. It is the process of allowing the meat to hang for prolonged periods of time. This achieves two things. First, it improves and intensifies the flavour of the steak. As moisture in the steak reduces, the intensity of flavour concentrates. Once you age steak to the 40-day and beyond mark, you start to get layers of new flavour. A well-aged steak carries an almost blue-cheese flavour. It's not for everyone, but for us they really punch above their weight in the flavour department.

The second result of dry aging is tenderness. Steaks that haven't been hung at all are generally a bit tough and chewy. The hanging process allows the enzymes and proteins in the meat to slowly break down in a controlled way.

When looking for dry aging, you need a minimum of 21 days, but for us the sweet spot is between 40 and 80 days.

THICKNESS

If you ever have the choice of two regular-sized steaks or one big thick one, go with the big thick one every time. It's far easier to focus on cooking one thick steak and nailing it than it is to cook multiple. And, the thickness allows you to build up crust on the steak without it overcooking.

Thin steaks are generally a waste of time. They are too thin to get a decent crust before being overcooked, leaving you with two options: an under-seared steak cooked medium-rare, or a well-seared steak that's well done and tough as old boots. Thickness wins with a steak every time. We like ours around the 5–6cm (2–2½-inch) mark. Once you start going above 7.5cm (3 inches), you're almost moving into roasting-joint territory.

PREPPING YOUR STEAK

You don't have to do all these steps every time you cook a steak, and you can cook a great steak ignoring the majority of them, but if you really want to make the effort, mix and match and try out a few.

SCORE THE FAT AND ROUGH IT UP

If you want to put the effort in, try scoring the fat and roughing the steak up. It may seem counterintuitive to purchase a beautiful cut and then start hacking into it, but trust us, it works.

Scoring the fat: take your knife and slice diagonally one way along the fat, then change angle and slice diagonally again, creating a criss-cross. This makes it quicker and easier to render the fat and stops it from contracting and curling the steak up. It also increases the surface area of the fat cap, which brings more caramelization and flavour, as well as helping the fat to render more quickly.

Roughing up the steak: take a sharp knife and make numerous small slices along the flesh. Don't cut too deep, you just want to give the steak a rough surface. Think of roughing up a roast potato – that rough surface increases the outer surface area and increases the crust. Those little slits will become gnarly, caramelized and delicious. More texture means more crust and more flavour.

DRY BRINE OVERNIGHT

See page 27 for a full explanation on dry brining. For us it's an essential step with steak. We like to season simply with flaked sea salt, cracked black pepper and garlic granules. Liberally season all over, then place the steak on a tray on a wire rack, uncovered, in the fridge overnight to dry the surface. This process of air-drying overnight helps your steak on its way to achieving the most glorious crust.

BRING YOUR STEAK UP TO ROOM TEMPERATURE FIRST?

I think this is b*llocks. No matter which steak cooking technique you use, you will at some point be using a high heat, and at some point a low heat. In all methods I think you get the best results when the steak has taken the longest time to cook. You are building flavour, the meat is relaxing, the juices are flowing. Having the steak at room temperature makes it cook more quickly, meaning more chance of overcooking it and less time slowly coming up to temperature. I always cook my steaks straight out of the fridge onto the grill, or with a few minutes out of the fridge, so that the outer area of the steak is at room temperature, but the core is still cold.

BASTE!

Basting doesn't just add flavour, it helps develop that all-important crust. For more information on how to make a basting brush and your basting liquor, see page 28.

When to baste? Best practice is to baste as soon as you flip your steak. When you flip the seared side, you should hopefully see a crust forming, and the all-important fat dancing – those little specks of fat jumping up and down. At that point you need to hit it with your baste. The baste will mix with the meat juices and rendered fat and start to bind to the meat. Flip again, baste again, and just keep building those layers of basted flavour.

THE 2-SECOND HAND RULE: GET YOUR COALS, GAS OR WOOD HOT!

Whatever you are cooking on, make sure when it comes to searing your steak that your cooking area is red hot. You should only be able to hold your hand over the grill for around 2 seconds before pulling away because it's too hot (see page 32).

KEEP THAT STEAK MOVING!

This is a grilling technique and our favourite way to cook steaks or chops. Traditionally, chefs were always trained to place meat on a hot grill and leave it. Give it a quarter turn for grill marks, flip, repeat.

Now, there is some visual joy in those aesthetically pleasing grill marks. But, for us, grill marks are a sign of failure when cooking steak. Think about it, crust is flavour. Why would you only want that flavour in a few lines around your steak? We want crust all over.

So, keep your steak moving. As soon as you chuck it on the grill, move it. Flip it. Chase that sizzle around the grill. Don't let any side stay too long. Keep flipping, keep basting, keep moving, and sear all the sides, top, bottom, edges. Baste every time you flip to build up that crust.

BOARD DRESSING!

We love to dress our chopping boards before slicing our steaks. For full details on this, head over to page 104.

If there's one guaranteed way to start an argument, it's discussing politics at a family function. The second-best way is that age-old question: what's the best way to cook a steak? To understand this, you firstly have to recognize what you are aiming for in the first place.

CRUST

A great steak needs a great crust. The crust serves two purposes: one, it gives your steak variance in texture between the rich crust and the tender, juicy meat inside. Two, it brings that umami hit and, if you've cooked it right, layers and layers of flavour.

TENDERNESS

Sometimes this can be out of your hands. I've cooked steaks that looked great on paper but were disappointing once cooked. I've also cooked the occasional bog-standard supermarket steak and it's been mind-blowing. Sometimes it's the luck of the draw. But there are definite techniques and processes we can use to help a steak along to be beautifully melt-in-the-mouth tender.

PERFECT PINK

This is something we became very strict about when we first started cooking steaks at our BBQs. What the hell is 'perfect pink'? Well, perfect pink refers to what we want to see when we cut a steak: a beautiful crust with pink meat the whole way through.

A badly cooked steak is when you slice it to reveal a thick line of grey, well-done meat on the outside with a raw or rare centre. People will claim this is medium-rare when, in fact, it's a steak that's well done on the outside and at best rare in the middle, at worst raw. This happens because the chef has hit the steak with too high a heat for too long, overcooking the outside while not giving the heat time to work through the steak and cook the centre evenly.

What we are after with perfect pink is a rich, delicious crust and, under the surface, the perfect doneness the whole way through. (Let's be clear here: perfect doneness is going to be from rare to medium. If you want your steak cooked any more than that, please skip this section of the book and maybe think about cooking chicken or perhaps some low-and-slow meats instead... or maybe just order a takeaway?)

FLAVOUR

At the end of the day, the most important aspect. We can forgive a bit of extra chew or a patchy crust if the flavour knocks you round the head, ties you up and sends you on a one-way trip to flavour town. This doesn't necessarily mean throwing all sorts of marinades and spices onto a steak. More often than not, that's the exact opposite of what you want to do with a nice piece of beef. For me, it's about building flavour that complements the meat, and seasoning steaks the right way.

Traditionally in the UK (and by traditionally, I mean the 1980s), your dad would grab a steak, whack it on a disposable BBQ, completely incinerate the outside with flames and lighter fluid, then remove it when he'd lost interest, run out of beer, or *Bullseye* was on. There was then a 50/50 chance it was edible. Would it be raw? Would it be overcooked? Who knew until you cut it open.

These days there are many techniques and many methods to cook a great steak. As the saying goes, 'There's more than one way to skin a cat.' I'm not sure I believe that, and honestly who is out there skinning cats on such a regular basis that they've developed a series of techniques for it? Cruella de Vil, maybe?

In the modern lexicon of BBQ cooking, there is one method that has become king for steak: reverse sear. So, let's talk about it.

REVERSE SEAR

It's overrated.

There, I've said it. I realize this is controversial in the BBQ world. It's the equivalent of saying you think the Beatles' back-catalogue is a bit 'meh' or that *The Last Jedi* was the best of the *Star Wars* films. Fans of reverse sear can border on religious zealotry. If you don't believe me, go online, find a BBQ group or forum and tell them reverse sear isn't the best way to cook a steak. You'll likely be bullied, berated and cast out like the heretical heathen you are.

But for me, it isn't the best way to cook a steak. I'll occasionally use the technique, especially if I fancy adding a bit of smoke flavour, but in general I find it's never quite as good as forward sear or sear-pause-repeat.

WHAT ARE REVERSE SEAR, FORWARD SEAR AND SEAR-PAUSE-REPEAT?

All three of these techniques rely on two different cooking temperatures: searing at an incredibly hot temperature, but cooking the meat at a very low temperature.

- Forward sear: searing your meat at a high temperature to develop its crust, then finishing it at a low temperature to cook it evenly.
- Reverse sear: cooking a steak until it's almost at your desired doneness, letting it cool down, then searing at a hot temperature to create a crust.

- Sear-pause-repeat: a combination of the two, searing your steak, removing it from the heat, resting it, then searing again.

All three techniques have pros and cons; which is best depends on the steak, how many you are cooking and what you feel like doing on the day. All three will work, and all three can give amazing results.

Try them out, see what you think. If you are as nerdy as we are, buy 3 identical steaks and try them each way and see which you prefer. Avoid dogma; never be told 'this is the only way' to do whatever. Fiercely sticking to and not questioning certain beliefs or practices is what leads to stagnation; pushing against tradition is where innovation lies and, most importantly, pick the technique that works best for you.

HOW TO FORWARD SEAR

Get your heat source going. This ideally should be whole chunks of wood burnt down to glowing embers, or lumpwood/briquettes that have reached optimum temperature. (This technique works fine on a gas BBQ, but you'll lack the inherent flavour you get from wood or charcoal.) Get your fire to the point where you can only hold your hand over it for 2 seconds before having to remove it. Then add your grill grates. Adding them too early can cause them to get so hot they scorch or burn the steak, which we don't want.

Once ready, take your fridge-cold steak (there's no need to bring it to room temperature; in fact, with forward sear, the colder the better as it slows down internal cooking). Start searing your steak, moving and basting to build as much crust as possible.

When the crust is where you want it, check the internal temperature. If your steak is thick enough, it should only be in the late 20s to mid-30s°C/80–95°F. Remove it from the direct heat and place it on a much cooler part of the grill. I like to finish my steaks extremely low, with an ambient temperature of roughly my desired finished doneness, generally 52–55°C/125–131°F.

You can achieve this best by distance from the heat source. If you're lucky enough to have a Santa Maria-style grill (see page 18), lift the steak high above the coals. This is a great opportunity to throw on a chunk of wood and let a little smoke lick the steak. Finishing it low like this means there's no need to rest the steak; it has been cooking and resting at the same time. It also means it's almost impossible to overcook, as the low ambient temperature removes the risk of carryover cooking.

PROS

- Lets you build as much crust as possible
- No need to rest the steak
- Finishing in extremely low ambient temperature minimizes the chance of overcooking
- Generally one load of fuel is enough, as the initial high heat and gradual decline mirror the cook stages
- The meat spends longer at higher temperature than reverse sear, giving collagen and fat more time to render

CONS

- Crust may not be as even as reverse sear (you can mitigate this with a good dry brine and fridge-drying)
- You will be a pariah in the BBQ world when you realize this technique is better than reverse sear
- The steak can take a long time to reach core temperature, and you may have drunk all of your beer.

HOW TO REVERSE SEAR

Set your BBQ or smoker to run at around 120°C/250°F – or you can go lower if desired. This is the opportunity to add a little wood. I'm not a fan of overly smoky steaks; I like mine to taste like beef, with subtle hints of smoke to complement rather than overpower.

Let your steak gently come up to temperature. When it hits 40–45°C/104–113°F, remove it and let it rest. We want the temperature to fall, giving more leeway to build that exterior crust. Resting could be anywhere from 10 minutes to an hour.

While the steak rests, fire up your heat source until it's screaming hot (2-second hand rule again). Apply your grill grate and start searing. Now here's the tricky part: with reverse sear you're in the danger zone. Internally the steak is in the high 30s to mid-40s°C/100–113°F. If you over-sear, you risk it going over. The high heat produces an amazing crust, but that same heat will want to push through the meat. Carryover cooking is a real factor.

If your target doneness is 55°C/131°F, pull it at 50–51°C/122–124°F. As it rests, the residual heat will continue cooking. After about 10 minutes your steak should be ready to slice.

PROS

- Low cooking at the start allows subtle smoke flavour
- Low cooking dries the surface of the meat, making crust development easier
- Fat has more time to warm and begin rendering

CONS

- Already in the 'danger zone' when searing, so it's easy to overcook
- Misjudging carryover cooking can ruin it (too raw or too done)
- Requires more wood or charcoal for a second high-heat phase

SEAR-PAUSE-REPEAT

This technique is brilliant for building up crust. Set your BBQ for 2-zone grilling. Once it's at optimum temperature (2-second hand rule), get your steaks on. Constantly move and baste them, letting the crust build, then remove to the cool zone or even off the grill entirely.

The steak won't stop cooking, but resting it away from the high heat allows the warmth inside to gently and evenly transfer through. After 5 minutes or so, return the steak to the hot grill, flipping and basting. After a few minutes, remove it to rest again. Probe it every time.

The number of times you repeat this depends on steak thickness. You want it 4–5°C/39–42°F below target when resting after the final sear. Carryover cooking during rest will bring it up to your desired temperature. Always flip while resting, so juices distribute evenly.

PROS

- Incredible crust development
- Constant attention gives more control

CONS

- Labour-intensive, more hands-on than forward or reverse sear
- More searing time can increase risk of overcooking

I believe it was American pitmaster Adam Perry Lang who pioneered this technique, and since I learned it, it's been something I do at home all the time for pretty much every steak (or chop) I cook. The best thing about seasoning the board is how versatile and open to interpretation it can be. You can be as minimal or as outlandish as you want, and it's just another way of giving the meat as much special care and attention as it deserves.

The whole concept behind seasoning the board is to give your piece of meat that extra little flourish at the end, that extra kick of flavour that takes you from a great steak to a life-changing steak. We are going to take our chopping board and load it with flavour: oils, aromatics, herbs. It's all going to be layered up so that when we throw the steak on top of the board, the heat of the steak starts to bring those flavours alive. As we move the steak around, the flavours soak in, building layer upon layer of flavour into the meat. Once it's sliced, the juices will mix with the dressing, creating even more amazing flavour. Enough talk, here's how to do it.

BASIC BOARD DRESSING

INGREDIENTS

OIL This can be olive oil, rapeseed oil, or even flavoured oil like garlic or chilli. Smoked oil is amazing for this. You can even use rendered beef fat or bone marrow (see the recipe on page 112).

GARLIC Either a whole head cut in half, or a clove for grating.

ONION Either a whole onion cut in half, or half an onion for grating.

HERBS Rosemary and thyme for beef, oregano and sage for pork, mint for lamb. Whatever takes your fancy. You can even use the ends from your herb basting brush (see page 28).

TECHNIQUE

Take your chopping board and cover it with a generous amount of whatever oil or fat you've decided to use. Grate your garlic and onion half onto the oil (or if using halves, rub the cut side directly onto the oiled board). Next, take your herbs (or the tips of your herb basting brush) and finely chop them.

Once your steak or chop is ready to serve, place the hot cut of meat on top of the board, moving it around as much as possible to cover every edge and side in the board dressing. When ready to slice, cut the meat as you desire, tossing the slices in the board dressing. Any juices released from the meat will mix with the dressing, and as you toss the slices, they'll soak that flavour straight back up.

Alternatively, leave your meat nicely sliced and serve your dressed steak to your guests directly on the dressed board, encouraging them to drag their slices through the dressing.

Board dressings are perfect for kitchen creativity. Try grating some chilli on there if you want spice. If you're cooking pork, grate a bit of lemon zest. A bit of freshly grated horseradish could make a cut of rump really sing. Experiment, try combos out, it's all about giving your meat the respect it deserves.

Serves: 4–6

BBQ setup: 2-zone direct grilling

Fuel source: Lumpwood, briquettes, or wood burnt down to embers

Cook time: 35–40 minutes, plus optional overnight dry brining

INGREDIENTS

1 whole bavette steak

Salt and ground black pepper or SPG (salt, pepper, garlic granules; see page 33)

For the Marmite butter baste

100g (scant ½ cup) salted butter

2 garlic cloves, peeled and squashed to release the flavour

2 tsp Marmite

1 herb basting brush (see page 28)

The Marmite baste on this is insane. It works with any cut of beef and doesn't scream 'Marmite' – it just makes the steak taste more, er… steaky. That deep, savoury, meaty hit you can't quite put your finger on.

Bavette is a great cut for BBQ. It's cheap, cooks quickly, and while it's not as tender as your fancier steaks, it more than makes up for it in the flavour department.

Season your steak generously, ideally the night before for a dry brine in the fridge.

Set your BBQ up for 2-zone direct grilling.

To make the baste, melt the butter in a small pan over a gentle heat, add the garlic cloves and Marmite and stir until combined. Keep it warm and ready for basting.

Oil up your grill grates and place the bavette directly over the searing hot coals. Sear for 1–2 minutes per side, moving it every few seconds to build up a crust.

Flip the steak and immediately start basting with your Marmite butter, using the herb brush. Keep flipping, basting and turning until you've built up a deep, dark, glossy crust.

Once you're happy with the colour, move the steak to the cooler side of the grill to finish gently. Remove it when it hits 52–55°C/125–131°F internal temperature. Note: bavette can be uneven in thickness, so if the thicker part is taking longer, fold the thinner parts above it to even out the cook.

Let the steak rest for a few minutes, then slice against the grain. For an extra umami kick, brush the slices with any leftover Marmite butter.

Serves: 1–2

BBQ setup: 2-zone direct grilling

Fuel source: Lumpwood, briquettes, or wood burnt down to embers

Cook time: 30 minutes, plus overnight dry brining

INGREDIENTS

1 large ribeye steak (600g–1kg/1lb 5oz–2lb 4oz), 2.5–5cm (1–2 inches) thick

SPG (salt, pepper, garlic granules; see page 33)

1 herb basting brush (see page 28)

Basting liquor (melted butter, garlic, rosemary and thyme; see page 28)

For the smoked Brit churri

½ red onion

3 beef fat confit garlic cloves (or 1 large fresh garlic clove)

Handful of flat-leaf parsley

1 tbsp red wine vinegar

1 tsp smoked salt

80ml (⅓ cup) rapeseed (canola) or olive (non-virgin) oil

40ml (⅙ cup) water

1 tsp English mustard

1 tsp cracked black pepper

The mighty ribeye. Arguably the people's choice when it comes to steak – it's fatty, it's flavourful, it's the most sought-after cut on the whole animal. In this recipe we're pairing it with Brit churri, our take on the classic Argentinian steak sauce chimichurri.

The origins of chimichurri are hotly debated, but for the purpose of this book we're going with one particular take. The story goes that chimichurri originates from British military officers who had become huge fans of curry while serving in India. When in Argentina, they supposedly asked their hosts for a spicy sauce, saying 'Gimme curry.' Is it true? Probably not. But it's a cool story.

We've Anglicized our chimichurri here by swapping out chilli flakes for fiery English mustard, giving it that Brit twist. If you haven't tried chimichurri before, you absolutely should. The real deal would also work well with this.

Prep your steak. Dry-brine your ribeye with SPG the night before cooking, leaving it uncovered in the fridge.

Cook the steak. Get your grill up to temperature. Sear your ribeye following whichever steak cooking method you prefer (see pages 100–102). For ribeye, aim for an internal temperature of around 55–56°C/131–133°F. There's a lot of fat in this cut, so cooking it a touch further than you might a sirloin or fillet really helps to get that fat rendering; you don't want it too rare.

Make the Brit churri. While the steak cooks, finely dice the onion and confit garlic. Add to a small jar (jam jar, Kilner jar, anything with a lid that won't melt). Finely chop the parsley and mix it in, along with all the remaining ingredients.

Smoke it. Take a small lump of red-hot coal from your BBQ, blow off any excess ash and carefully drop it into the jar. It will start smoking instantly. Slam the lid on and trap that smoke inside. Let it infuse for about a minute, then remove the coal.

Serve. Slice your ribeye and serve it with a good spoonful of smoky, tangy Brit churri on the side.

Serves: 1–2

BBQ setup: 2-zone direct grilling

Fuel source: Lumpwood, briquettes, or wood burnt down to embers

Cook time: 45 minutes, plus optional overnight dry brining

INGREDIENTS

1 T-bone steak, 900g–1.2kg (2lb–2lb 12oz), 4–5cm (1½–2 inches) thick

SPG (salt, pepper, garlic granules; see page 33)

1 herb basting brush (see page 28)

Basting liquor (melted butter, garlic, rosemary and thyme; see page 28)

Dirty Diane sauce (see page 216)

You've got to love a T-bone. For me, it's the best-looking steak. With a T-bone, there's a T-shaped bone (hence the name) and on the one side a sirloin, and on the other side a little fillet steak. Two steaks in one. How awesome is that?

And then there's Diane sauce. It's a classic with good reason. Here, we've given it a Beefy Boys upgrade, with smoked garlic and a cheeky bit of Bovril.

Get the steak on. Season your steak with SPG, ideally the night before to let it dry-brine uncovered in the fridge.

When ready to cook, set your BBQ up for 2-zone direct grilling. Once it's hot enough that you can only hold your hand over the grill for 2 seconds, you're good to go. So get oiling the grill grates.

Place the T-bone on the grill fat-side down first, letting that fat start to render. Move the steak around every 2 minutes so the fat gets an even cook. After about 4–6 minutes, sear the rest of the steak, constantly flipping and basting to build up that all-important crust. Watch the fillet side, it'll overcook faster than the sirloin.

Once the crust looks great, move the steak to the cooler zone. Keep the fat cap facing the fuel so the fillet side is further away from the heat and less likely to overcook.

Make the Dirty Diane sauce. While the steak finishes, follow the instructions on page 216.

Finish the steak. Probe the steak. For me, 52°C/125°F is perfect. If the cool zone of your grill is running low and gentle, take it off at 52°C/125°F and rest briefly. If it's hotter, pull it off at 49–50°C/120–122°F and let carryover heat bring it up to temperature. The sirloin side can happily run into the mid-50s°C/130s°F, but I wouldn't take the fillet much higher than 52°C/125°F.

Carve by running your knife down along the bone to remove the sirloin and fillet in one piece each. Slice against the grain and lay the slices back out around the bone. Once sliced, give your steak a sprinkle of coarse rock salt.

Serve with the Dirty Diane sauce on the side.

Serves: 1–2

BBQ setup: 2-zone direct grilling

Fuel source: Lumpwood, briquettes, or wood burnt down to embers

Cook time: 1 hour, plus optional overnight dry brining

INGREDIENTS

500g (1lb 2oz) sirloin steak

Salt and ground black pepper or SPG (salt, pepper, garlic granules; see page 33)

1 split bone marrow

A little chopped fresh thyme and rosemary

Basting liquor (melted butter and garlic; see page 28)

1 garlic clove

½ white onion

1 lemon, for zesting

Coarse rock salt (smoked if you like) and cracked black pepper

We've already talked about dressing the board when it comes to a steak (see page 104). This takes that concept and makes it extra boujee with the addition of bone marrow. Feel free to switch out the sirloin; this works amazingly well with fillet, flat iron, or any other steak that's lighter in the fat department. The bone marrow board dressing just brings an incredible extra hit of richness.

Season in advance. Ideally season your steak the night before and leave it uncovered in the fridge to dry brine and dry out.

Roast the bone marrow. Set up your grill for 2-zone cooking. Once up to temperature, season your split bone with smoked salt, pepper, thyme and rosemary. Place it in the cool zone, lid on, and roast until the marrow is cooked through (about 15 minutes). Keep the bones warm by moving them to a cooler part of the grill.

Cook the steak. Sear the steak directly over the coals, moving and basting it constantly with your basting butter (using your basting brush) to build up a beautiful crust. Once you've got your desired crust, move it to the cool zone, turning and basting every few minutes until it reaches your preferred doneness (52°C/125°F is perfect for me). Or, if you fancy, follow one of the other steak cooking methods on pages 100–102.

Dress the board. Move quickly here – once the marrow cools it will coagulate, and you want it while it's still nice and hot. Grate the garlic and onion directly onto your chopping board. Scoop the bone marrow out of the bones and drop it on top. Chop the herbs from the end of your basting brush over the marrow, grate over some lemon zest and finish with a good pinch of coarse rock salt and a twist of black pepper. Use your knife to chop everything together into a rich, aromatic paste.

Finish and serve. Take your hot steak and roll it through the bone marrow mix – the heat from the meat will wake up the garlic and onion. Slice the steak and drag the slices through the marrow dressing before chowing down.

Serves: 2–4
BBQ setup: 2-zone direct grilling
Fuel source: Lumpwood, briquettes, or wood burnt down to embers
Cook time: 40 minutes, plus overnight dry brining

INGREDIENTS

1 bone-in ribeye (800g–1kg/ 1lb 12oz–2lb 4oz) – although any good-quality steak will work
SPG (salt, pepper, garlic granules; see page 33)
1 herb basting brush (see page 28)
2 whole lobsters

For the Beefy Boy butter

150g (⅔ cup) salted butter
3 smoked garlic cloves (see page 154; regular garlic also works)
1 shallot
1 red chilli
1 tbsp capers
Handful of parsley
Handful of chives
Zest and juice of 1 lemon
½ tsp English mustard
1 tsp creamed horseradish

It's rare to see a combo of such icons, both at the top of their game, this strong. So rare, in fact, that the only parallels I can think of are Dre and Eminem, Deadpool and Wolverine, or the Chuckle Brothers.

Surf and Turf always needs a sauce that can work with both proteins, and tie them together. Beefy Boy Butter is just that. It's my absolute favourite compound butter recipe, and it works as well with fish as it does with meat. It's a goddamn powerhouse of a butter.

Prep the steak. Season your ribeye with SPG the night before so it has plenty of time to dry brine and absorb all the seasoning.

Make the butter. Melt the butter in a pan. Finely chop the garlic, shallot, chilli, capers and fresh herbs and mix them into the melted butter. Cook until the garlic and shallot have softened, then add the lemon zest and juice, mustard and horseradish. This is your Beefy Boy butter.

Cook the steak. Get your grill up to temperature for 2-zone cooking. Sear the ribeye over direct heat, using the herb brush to baste with the Beefy Boy butter as you go, to build up that crust. Once it's looking good, move it over to the cooler side of the grill to finish slowly. (Or follow any of the steak cooking methods on pages 100–102 if you've got a favourite.)

Cook the lobster. Split the whole lobster straight down the middle and season with SPG. Place directly onto the grill, flesh-side down, for about 3–4 minutes to get some colour. Flip onto the shell side and baste generously with Beefy Boy butter. Put the lid on the BBQ and cook until the lobster reaches an internal temperature of 57°C/134°F in the thickest part. Remove from the grill and keep warm.

Finish the steak. Once your ribeye hits 56–57°C/133–134°F, take it off and let it rest briefly. Slice it off the bone, then cut against the grain.

Serve. Plate the steak slices with the lobster and plenty of Beefy Boy butter for dipping.

Serves: 2–4

BBQ setup: 2-zone direct grilling

Fuel source: Lumpwood, briquettes, or wood burnt down to embers

Cook time: 40 minutes, plus optional overnight dry brining

INGREDIENTS

A nice thick rump steak, 900g (2lb)

1 herb basting brush (see page 28)

Basting liquor (melted butter, garlic, rosemary and thyme; see page 28)

Salt and ground black pepper, or SPG (salt, pepper, garlic granules; see page 33)

For the anchovy hollandaise

2 egg yolks

10 anchovy fillets in oil

1 garlic clove, peeled

Juice of ½ lemon

200g (generous ¾ cup) melted butter

Salt and ground black pepper

Back in the 80s and 90s, if we're leaning into stereotypes, it was law in the UK that any dad going for a pub meal would order rump steak and chips. In recent times it's been massively overshadowed by much flashier alternatives. Rump has a reputation for being chewy and lacking in flavour, but cook one right and it's a different story. We like to channel our inner 80s dad by serving this with low-and-slow grilled tomatoes and mushrooms (see the veg platter on page 148, and cook the mushrooms using the same method as the tomatoes) and our live-fire chips (fries) on page 58.

So whack on some Dire Straits, grow a moustache and cook yourself some slap-up rump.

Take a sharp knife and make criss-crosses in the fat of the steak, then season it up! (Ideally do this the night before.)

Set your BBQ up for 2-zone grilling and get the grill raging hot (see the 2-second hand rule on page 32). Oil up your grill grate, then place the steak fat side down directly on the grill. Let the fat render for a good 4–5 minutes, watching it doesn't burn. Once you have some good colour on the fat, it's time to lay the steak on its side. Keep it moving around, building up that crust, then flip it after 2–3 minutes and baste it. Repeat this process until you've built up colour and crust all over your steak.

When you're happy with the crust, move the steak over to the cooler side of the grill, keeping the fat pointed towards the heat. Let the steak finish off slowly – you want to be taking your rump off the grill around the 52–54°C/125–129°F internal temperature mark. Remove and leave to rest while you make the anchovy hollandaise.

Add the egg yolks, anchovies, garlic and lemon juice to a food processor and blitz to create a paste. Now slowly trickle in the melted butter with the processor still whizzing. This should give you a beautifully thick and creamy hollandaise.

Serve the rump and sauce alongside a roasted tomato and mushroom, and our chips from page 58. For extra dad points, play Phil Collins mega loud, have it with a can of your favourite beer and fall asleep in your chair after.

Serves: 2–4

BBQ setup: 2-zone direct grilling

Fuel source: Lumpwood, briquettes, or wood burnt down to embers

Cook time: 45 minutes, plus overnight dry brining

INGREDIENTS

1 large porterhouse steak (1–1.5kg/2lb 4oz–3lb 5oz), cut from the thicker end of the loin

SPG (salt, pepper, garlic granules; see page 33)

1 herb basting brush (see page 28)

Basting liquor (melted butter, garlic, rosemary and thyme; see page 28)

1 loaf of beef fat bread (see page 78) or a good-quality focaccia/ciabatta

1 quantity of beef fat confit garlic (see page 155), and the beef fat it was cooked in, for brushing

Coarse rock salt, to finish

Smoked Brit churri (see page 108) or your favourite steak sauce/compound butter, to serve

So, what exactly is a porterhouse? It is in fact the bigger, badder brother of the T-bone. If your T-bone has a chunky fillet side, chances are it's actually a porterhouse. With a proper Fred Flintstone vibe, the porterhouse is also perfect for sharing, which is how we serve it here.

Prep the steak. For a steak this size (4–5cm/1½–2 inches thick), you'll definitely want to dry-brine the night before, seasoning with SPG and leaving it uncovered in the fridge. It's a big hunk of meat and you need that seasoning working its way deep inside, not just sitting on the surface.

Get grilling. Fire up your BBQ for 2-zone cooking. Start by searing the fat cap until it begins to render. Flip the steak onto its sides and start building that crust, using the herb basting brush and basting liquor.

Finish low and slow. Once the crust is formed, move the steak to the cooler side of the grill. Let the ambient heat finish the cook, turning and basting as you go. (Alternatively, follow one of the other steak cooking methods on pages 100–102.)

After searing, keep the fillet as far away from the heat source as possible. Ideally, the fillet should finish a few degrees behind the sirloin – the target internal temperature is 52–55°C/125–131°F.

Toast the bread. While the steak finishes, slice your bread into 1.5cm (⅝-inch) slabs. Toast over the direct heat, brushing with the garlic beef fat from your confit.

Load it up. Once toasted, spread the confit garlic cloves over the bread and sprinkle with a pinch of coarse salt.

Slice the steak. When the porterhouse is ready, carve along both sides of the T-bone to remove the fillet and sirloin. Slice against the grain. Brush the slices with a little of that infused beef fat, if you like, and add a sprinkle of coarse salt.

Serve. Arrange the toasted bread around the steak, then take a slice and place it on the bread. Add a dollop of Brit churri or your chosen sauce/butter.

Serves: 6–8

BBQ setup: Rotisserie

Fuel source: Lumpwood or briquettes

Cook time: 25–30 minutes, plus optional 24-hour dry brining

1 picanha, about 1.5kg (3lb 5oz)

Salt and coarsely ground black pepper, or SPG (salt, pepper, garlic granules; see page 33)

For the wild garlic butter

Handful of flat-leaf parsley leaves

Good handful of wild garlic leaves, or 2 garlic cloves

200g (generous ¾ cup) salted butter, softened

Wild garlic is one of the best things about spring. I get great pleasure from dragging my family around the countryside looking for green gold. If you cannot get wild garlic, do not worry, this works just as well with regular garlic.

Picanha is amazing – cut from the rump, it works beautifully on the rotisserie. You get that gorgeous fat cap and the super-tender rump underneath.

Prep your meat, ideally the night before. There are two ways to slice your picanha and the decision you make now determines how you slice it once it is cooked. If you want long, thin slices at the end, cut the raw picanha against the grain when portioning. If you want chunky strips once cooked, cut the raw picanha along the grain when portioning.

Portion the triangle-shaped picanha into 3 or 4 steaks using the along-the-grain or against-the-grain technique depending on how you want to carve it later. Season all over with salt and pepper or SPG.

To make the wild garlic butter, finely chop the parsley and wild garlic, or crush the regular garlic cloves, and mix with the softened butter.

Set your BBQ up for rotisserie cooking. Once your coals are ready, spear the picanha steaks onto the rotisserie rod and load it up. Start basting with the wild garlic butter as the steaks turn on the spit, and continue basting as they cook.

As soon as the picanha hits between 52 and 55°C/125 and 131°F internal temperature, take off the heat and let rest.

Carve the picanha, being mindful of the grain direction based on how you prepped it. Brush your slices with more melted wild garlic butter and enjoy.

Serves: 2

BBQ setup: 2-zone direct grilling

Fuel source: Lumpwood, briquettes, or wood burnt down to embers

Cook time: 35–40 minutes, plus optional overnight dry brining

INGREDIENTS

2 porkerhouse chops, about 4cm (1½ inches) thick (ask your butcher for a pork chop that has both the tenderloin and the top loin, and to remove the rind and crosshatch the fat that is left)

Salt and ground black pepper, or SPG (salt, pepper, garlic granules; see page 33)

A little dried thyme, rosemary, sage or fennel seeds (optional)

For the rhubarb and mustard ketchup

½ tbsp butter

1 onion, roughly chopped

200g (7oz) rhubarb, cut into batons

1½ tbsp light brown sugar

80ml (⅓ cup) water

1½ tbsp golden syrup

2 tsp salt

1 tsp English mustard

You would be forgiven for thinking that the combination of rhubarb and mustard are only included in this book because mustard rhymes with custard. There may be some merit in that, but this really works. Rhubarb has a natural zing and fruitiness that pairs beautifully with mustard, and when you treat it like a ketchup it is dynamite on a slab of pork.

The porkerhouse here is based on taking the famous beef porterhouse and applying the same butchery, giving you a big, thick juicy chop with a good-sized fillet. For this recipe we are removing the rind – it's tricky to get great crackling on a pork chop and removing it allows you to concentrate on that creamy pork fat underneath, which can get super-caramelized and delicious.

Season your pork chops, ideally the day before, with just salt and pepper, or with SPG, or with extra herbs and spices.

To make the ketchup, melt the butter in a pan and sauté the onion and rhubarb until they are both soft. Place in a food processor with the remaining ketchup ingredients and blitz until smooth. Check the seasoning for salty, sweet and vinegary notes, adjust as needed and set aside.

Set your grill up for 2-zone direct grilling. Place the pork chops on the hot grill, fat-side down. You may need something to lean them against. Check every 2–3 minutes that the fat is not burning.

Once you are happy with the caramelization on the fat, it is time to lay the chops flat on the grill and sear, constantly moving them to colour the chop all over.

Once seared, place the chops on the cooler part of the grill with the fat facing the fire and the fillet side as far away from the heat as possible.

I like my pork relatively pink, so I take it off around 58°C/136°F, but if you prefer yours more done, aim for 65°C/149°F.

Let the chops rest for a minute or two, then tuck in with the rhubarb and mustard ketchup alongside.

Serves: 2–4

BBQ setup: 2-zone direct grilling

Fuel source: Lumpwood, briquettes, or wood burnt down to embers

Cook time: 30 minutes, plus overnight marinating

INGREDIENTS

4 double pork chops (2.5cm/ 1 inch thick; the thickness helps them stay juicy)

Blue Monday sauce (see page 215)

2 ripe pears

Salt and ground black pepper

For the marinade

8 ripe pears (seeds and stalks removed)

4 tbsp cider vinegar

1 tbsp salt

½ tbsp ground black pepper

½ tbsp thyme (fresh or dried)

½ tbsp rosemary (fresh or dried)

1 tbsp sage (fresh or dried)

1 tbsp sugar

4 garlic cloves, peeled

When it's cooked right, a good pork chop is up there with a great steak. Here, the natural enzymes in the pears help tenderize and flavour the meat, making it super-juicy and delicious.

Make the marinade. Peel and core the 8 pears. Blitz until smooth in a food processor with the remaining marinade ingredients.

Prep your pork chops. Take a sharp knife and score through the fat every 5mm (¼ inch) or so. This helps the fat render and crisp up during the cook. Or ask your butcher to do it for you. Place the pork in the marinade, cover and leave it in the fridge overnight.

Cook the pork. Set your grill up for 2-zone cooking. Once the grill is up to temperature (the classic 2-second hand rule, see page 32), brush any excess marinade off the chops and season lightly with salt and pepper – make sure you dry the pork fat and get plenty of salt on it.

Start fat-side down. Let the fat crisp up gently, checking regularly. If it's cooking too fast or looks like it might burn, move it away from the direct heat for a bit. After 4–5 minutes you should have rendered a good amount of fat out and built up some lovely colour.

Sear the chops on both sides over the high heat, making sure to get good colour all around. Once you're happy with the sear, move them to the cooler zone to finish slowly. Keep turning and probing until the internal temperature hits 62°C/143°F, then take them off the grill and let them rest for 5 minutes.

Make the Blue Monday sauce. Follow the instructions on page 215.

Grill the pears. Peel and core the 2 pears, and slice in half. Brush your grill lightly with oil and grill them over a medium heat until they're nicely charred and warmed through.

Serve. Pour the Blue Monday sauce into a bowl, slice your pork chop, and lay it on the side. Add the grilled pears on the side.

Serves: 4
BBQ setup: 2-zone direct grilling
Fuel source: Lumpwood, briquettes, or wood burnt down to embers
Cook time: 35–40 minutes, plus optional overnight dry brining

INGREDIENTS

4 Barnsley lamb chops
1 herb basting brush (see page 28)
Basting liquor (melted butter, garlic, rosemary, mint and lemon juice; see page 28)
Salt and ground black pepper

For the smoked mint churri
30g (1oz) mint leaves
1 garlic clove
1 small onion
1½ tbsp red wine vinegar
80ml (⅓ cup) oil
80ml (⅓ cup) water
1 tsp salt
½ tsp ground black pepper

In Barnsley, in Britain's South Yorkshire, sometime around the mid-1800s, local farmers were known for eating big, double-loin lamb chops, and when a stranger at a local inn came in asking for 'a big chop, a real chop... you know, a Barnsley chop,' the legend was born. They're epic cuts: soft, tender loin meat with a strip of belly attached, giving you beautiful melty lamb fat when cooked right.

Prep the lamb and BBQ. Score the fat on the back of each chop; season generously with salt and pepper, ideally the night before for a dry brine.

Set up your BBQ for direct grilling. Start with a low heat – the 8-second hand rule (see page 32). Oil your grill grates, then place the chops fat-side down. You may need to balance them against something, like a brick wrapped in foil, to keep them upright.

Cook slowly for around 20–25 minutes, checking regularly. The goal here is to gently render that belly fat until it's golden, crisp and tender.

Sear the meat. Once the fat is perfectly rendered, adjust your grill for high heat (2-second hand rule). Lay the chops flat on their side and sear for 1–2 minutes, moving them continuously to build up a crust.

Flip and baste as you go, using your herb brush to brush them with your basting liquor. Keep flipping and searing until the loins hit 57–58°C/134–136°F internal temperature, then take them off the heat and let them rest for a few minutes.

Make the smoked mint churri. Finely chop the mint, garlic and onion, and combine them in a jar with the vinegar, oil, water, salt and pepper.

Now for the fun bit. Take a small piece of red-hot coal (about 2–3cm/¾–1¼ inches square), blow off any excess ash and carefully place it in the jar. Smoke should start billowing straight away. Quickly put the lid on and let it smoke for a minute or two. Be careful: too much smoke can make it taste like an ashtray. We just want a hint.

Serve. Cut the loins off the bone, slice into strips and dice the belly into golden cubes. Spoon over your smoked mint churri and dig in.

Serves: 4–8

BBQ setup: 2-zone direct grilling

Fuel source: Lumpwood, briquettes, or wood burnt down to embers

Cook time: 30 minutes

INGREDIENTS

8 best end lamb chops

Salt and ground black pepper, or SPG (salt, pepper, garlic granules; see page 33)

Worcestershire sauce glaze (see page 217)

1 herb basting brush (see page 28)

These are so delicious and moreish. The best thing about a best end lamb chop is the bit of fatty rib meat connected to the loin. If you cook it right it just melts, and then you get the best of both worlds by having the beautifully pink loin meat to follow it up. The sticky Worcestershire glaze makes these like a sweet and sticky lamb chop lollipop (popsicle)... good lord it's a lolli-chop! (I am off to trademark that.)

Get your grill set up for 2-zone direct grilling over a medium heat. You should be able to hold your hand over the coals for about 4 seconds.

Prep your lamb chops by giving them a liberal seasoning all over.

To make the glaze, follow the instructions on page 217.

Now it's time to cook the lamb. Oil up your grill grates and place the lamb fat-side down. You may need something to rest the chops against, so they don't fall over. We want to slowly cook the fat side of the meat while protecting the loin. After 3 or 4 minutes, check the fat isn't burning. Place it back on the grill and continue to cook the fat for another 4–5 minutes.

When you are happy that you have rendered enough of the fat out, it's time to sear the sides of the chop. Increase the heat of your grill by either adding more fuel or lowering your grill grate closer to the coals. We are now looking for 2-second hand rule (see page 32).

Start to sear the side of the meat, moving it every few seconds. After a minute or so, flip it over and baste it with the Worcestershire glaze, using your herb brush. Repeat this until your chop is reading around 60°C/140°F in the loin.

At this point, take it off the heat and allow it to rest. Give it another good basting while you are at it. Once it has rested for 3 or 4 minutes it's time to tuck in, rib first!

Well, we can't do a Beefy Boys cookbook without doing some burgers, can we?

If you want to get full-on nerdy about the world of burgers and patty styles, we can highly recommend our first book, *The Beefy Boys: From Backyard BBQs to World-Class Burgers*, where we dive deep into every detail of burger-making over 224 pages of pure, unadulterated burger porn.

Our publishers tell us we can't just force you to go and buy that, and we need to recap the basics here. So strap in!

THE MEAT

80% lean to 20% fat. That's the golden ratio. Almost any cut of beef will work for burgers as long as you get the fat content right. A solid go-to blend is 50% chuck and 50% brisket. Chuck brings that classic beefy flavour, brisket brings the fat and richness.

ONLY SEASON THE OUTSIDE

Treat your beef patties like a steak. If you season the mix itself, you'll end up curing the meat and it'll go tough. Only season the outside of your patties, on the grill, after they have been smashed.

100% MEAT

A great patty needs nothing else. No breadcrumbs. No egg. No filler. Just high-quality meat, minced as fresh as possible. This isn't a meatloaf, mate.

SMASH AND COOK

You need a hotplate for this, whether it's a dedicated flat-top like a Weber Slate or Blackstone, or just a solid cast-iron plate thrown straight on the coals. What you want is a red-hot, flat cooking surface. Once it's around 220°C/430°F, it's time to smash. Place your balls of meat onto the grill and, using a spatula, smash the patty to your desired thickness. Season with SPG (see page 33). Once the edges are cooking and you see holes developing in the patty, it's time to flip. Use your spatula to make sure you get all the crust, and flip, then it's time to add cheese and steam.

THE STEAM

This is what makes a burger a **Beefy Boys Burger**. It's all about the steam.

Once your patties are cooking, add your cheese and bun lid on top. Then spray a little water directly onto the hotplate next to the burgers and cover them with a cloche. The steam will trap the heat and melt the cheese perfectly, while gently warming your bun. It's a little burger sauna, and it's glorious.

That's your whistle-stop tour of how to make a proper burger the Beefy Boys way. Follow those rules and you'll be fine. But if you want the full story, the techniques, the science, the waffle, go grab our first book.

Makes: Enough for 6–8 burgers

75ml (5 tbsp) milk
2 tsp sodium citrate
½ tsp salt
1 tbsp butter
200g (7oz) Cheddar
100g (3½oz) Red Leicester
(or Double Gloucester)

If I had to pick a hill to die on, it's the What Cheese is Best For a Burger Hill.

We use loads of different cheeses on burgers at Beefy's – Jack cheese, Swiss cheese, blue cheese, mozzarella – but the single best cheese for a burger? It's American cheese.

Yes, yes, we know.

'It isn't proper cheese.'
'That's plastic cheese.'

We've heard it all. And you're right – it's horrendous. It isn't real cheese. But when it comes to burgers, it's the best cheese by far. So why?

The real reason American cheese works so well is its low melting point and, just like the Rolling Stones or the Hulk's underpants, its refusal to split. There's nothing else quite like it.

But we get the naysayers, and what we're aiming to do here is meet them halfway – to make our own American-style cheese, using zero chemicals, real cheese, and a bit of time and effort to elevate our burger game.

We're going to achieve this with a little-known ingredient called sodium citrate, which sounds terrifying but is effectively just citrus salt. The reason we use it is because it breaks down cheese into a silky liquid when heated, and that's exactly what we want for our *British Burger Cheese.*

Add the milk, sodium citrate, salt and butter to a pan over a gentle heat and stir until everything is dissolved together.

Slice your cheeses up. I like to chuck mine in the microwave for about a minute after slicing to get the melting started; it's not essential, it just speeds the whole process up. Add your cheese to the milk mixture. Keep stirring and heating gently until it becomes a super-smooth, glossy cheese sauce.

Taste and check the seasoning. If it needs more salt, add it.

Now grab a tray and slowly pour the cheese into it, spreading it out to form a layer a few millimetres (⅛ inch) thick. Pop it in the fridge to set – overnight is ideal, but it'll be ready to use after about 30 minutes.

Once set, run a spatula underneath to loosen it, flip it onto a chopping board, and slice into perfect burger-sized squares.

And there you go, you've just made good, honest British burger cheese.

The best bit? You can use pretty much any cheese for this recipe. Fancy trying some Stinking Bishop? Go for it. Brie? Why not. Mini Babybel? Maybe leave that one.

Serves: 1

BBQ setup: 2-zone direct grilling, plus hotplate for the onions (and if doing smash burgers)

Fuel source: Lumpwood, briquettes, or wood burnt down to embers

Cook time: 10 minutes (plus smoking and braising the pulled chuck)

INGREDIENTS

170g (6oz) minced (ground) beef

Salt and ground black pepper, or SPG (salt, pepper, garlic granules; see page 33)

1 semi-brioche or potato burger bun

1 slice of white onion, about 8mm (⅜ inch) thick, kept together as one piece

1–2 dashes of malt vinegar

1 tsp beef dripping

1 slice of British burger cheese (see page 132)

100–150g (3½–5½oz) pulled and braised beef chuck (see page 48), and 1 side pot of the braising jus

For the beef and mustard mayo

225g (1 cup) mayonnaise

3 tsp English mustard

1 tsp Bovril

With this burger we wanted to embrace the traditional flavours of classic English grub. So we have beef, English mustard, onion, cheese, more beef, and gravy. The only way this burger could be more English would be if it got drunk and thrown off a Jet2 holiday.

This burger also slaps without the pulled beef. Like all the best burgers, it's simple, and you can let the flavours of the beef and toppings shine.

To make the beef and mustard mayo, combine the ingredients in a bowl and mix thoroughly.

Get your BBQ ready for 2-zone direct grilling plus hotplate. Season the minced beef with salt and ground black pepper, or SPG, then shape into a patty – any style works for this.

Toast your bun and spread the bottom half with the beef and mustard mayo.

Take your slice of white onion, season it and add the malt vinegar. Melt the beef dripping on the hotplate and fry the onion in the beef dripping. Be careful when you flip it to keep the onion slice intact. Once caramelized, place it on top of the mayo.

Cook the burger patty on the grill as directed on page 130, or go smoked (see page 142) if you want even more flavour, then add the slice of cheese and steam under a cloche to melt it. Place the beef patty on top of the onion. Place your pulled chuck on top.

Serve alongside a little pot of the cooking liquor from the braised beef.

You can now eat your burger like a true Englishman. Feel free to complain about the weather and form orderly queues.

Serves: 1

BBQ setup: 2-zone direct grilling (plus hotplate if doing smash burgers)

Fuel source: Lumpwood, briquettes, or wood burnt down to embers

Cook time: 20 minutes for the burger (plus cooking the haggis)

INGREDIENTS

Whisky mayo (see page 216)

170g (6oz) minced (ground) beef or lamb

Salt and ground black pepper, or SPG (salt, pepper, garlic granules; see page 33)

1 semi-brioche or potato burger bun

1 cooked haggis, sliced and reformed into a patty shape

For the pickled neeps

350–400g (10½–14oz) swede (rutabaga), peeled

1½ tbsp salt

1½ tbsp sugar

120ml (½ cup) white malt vinegar

480ml (2 cups) water

For the Mull of Kintyre burger cheese

250g (9oz) Mull of Kintyre cheese, diced

75ml (5 tbsp) milk

2 tsp sodium citrate

1 tsp salt

1 tbsp butter

Haggis is underrated. I love its peppery taste and texture – it's delicious and we should be eating it all over the UK. Scotland's a magical place; there's something regal about it. Beautiful buildings, landscapes, history, tradition. The Scottish have an edge and wit to them where you are never sure if they are threatening you or are your best mate, or both. Edinburgh during the Fringe festival might also be one of the greatest places on earth.

This burger is a full celebration of Scotland: haggis, Mull of Kintyre burger cheese, pickled neeps and a whisky mayo.

For the pickled neeps, slice the swede into thin squares (or spiralize it if you're feeling fancy) and place in a bowl. Gently heat the salt, sugar, vinegar and water in a pan until dissolved, bring to the boil, then remove from the heat. Pour the liquid over the swede and let it all cool. The neeps will pickle as they sit.

For the Mull of Kintyre burger cheese, add all the ingredients to a pan over a low heat. Heat gently, stirring until fully melted and smooth. Let cool slightly, then pour onto a baking tray to level out. Chill in the fridge – it will be usable within an hour, but is even better left overnight.

For the whisky mayo, follow the instructions on page 216 and set aside.

Season the minced beef or lamb with salt and ground black pepper, or SPG, then shape into a patty – any style works for this.

Get your BBQ ready for 2-zone direct grilling (or a hotplate if doing a smash burger). Cook the patty on the grill as directed on page 130, then add a slice of Mull of Kintyre cheese and steam under a cloche to melt it.

To build the burger, toast your bun and spread the whisky mayo on the bottom bun. Add a generous layer of pickled neeps. Place the patty on top of the neeps and crown it with the haggis patty. Put the lid on and get it in yer belly.

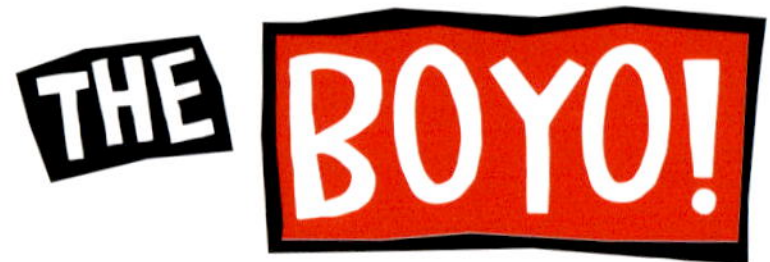

INGREDIENTS

170g (6oz) minced (ground) beef or lamb

Salt and ground black pepper, or SPG (salt, pepper, garlic granules; see page 33)

1 semi-brioche or potato burger bun

For the Welsh rarebit burger cheese

2 tsp sodium citrate

1 tbsp butter

1 tsp English mustard

2 tbsp Worcestershire sauce

1 tbsp bitter ale

200g (7oz) Black Bomber cheese, diced

For the bacon and leek jam

300g (10½oz) bacon lardons

2 leeks, finely chopped

1 tbsp white sugar

1 tbsp boiling water

For the laverbread patty

120g (4¼oz) canned laverbread

30g (1oz) oatmeal

1 tbsp bacon fat

Wales is a true gem of the British Isles, and I'm lucky to live right next to it. It's beautiful, and nowhere matches the sense of humour and warmth of the Welsh people. Beautiful country. Beautiful people.

Taking inspiration from the culinary delights of Cymru, we've built a burger that's pure Welsh chaos and comfort: Welsh rarebit burger cheese, a beef (or lamb) patty, a laverbread patty, and a bacon-and-leek jam. Tidy.

For the Welsh rarebit burger cheese, add all the ingredients to a saucepan. Warm gently over a low heat, stirring constantly – it will suddenly turn perfectly smooth and glossy.

Remove from the heat and let it cool slightly, then pour onto a tray and let it level out. Chill in the fridge for at least 1 hour (overnight is even better). Once firm, you can cut it into burger-sized slices.

For the bacon and leek jam, add the bacon lardons to a pan and cook over a medium-low heat until deeply caramelized and lots of fat has rendered.

Add the leeks and sauté for around 10 minutes until soft, sweet and fully cooked down. Add the sugar and boiling water and stir through. Remove from the heat and cool.

For the laverbread patty, mix the laverbread with the oatmeal. Shape 1 large patty or 2 small patties. Heat the bacon fat in a medium-hot frying pan, add the patty/patties and fry on both sides for 3–4 minutes, until cooked and crisp at the edges.

Season the minced beef or lamb with salt and ground black pepper, or SPG, then shape into a patty – any style works for this.

Get your BBQ ready for 2-zone direct grilling (or a hotplate if doing a smash burger). Cook the patty on the grill as directed on page 130, then add a slice of Welsh rarebit cheese and steam under a cloche to melt it.

To build your burger, toast your bun. Add a generous spoonful of bacon and leek jam to the bottom bun. Stack your laverbread patty/patties on top. Add the bun lid and tuck in.

Banging.

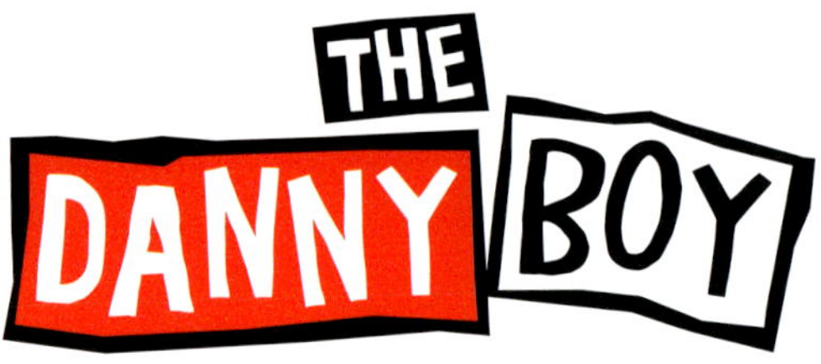

Serves: 1

BBQ setup: 2-zone direct grilling (plus hotplate if doing smash burgers)

Fuel source: Lumpwood, briquettes, or wood burnt down to embers

Cook time: 20 minutes for the burger (plus smoking the beef rib)

INGREDIENTS

Champ mayo (see page 216)

170g (6oz) minced (ground) beef or lamb

Salt and ground black pepper, or SPG (salt, pepper, garlic granules; see page 33)

1 semi-brioche or potato burger bun

1 Guinness-glazed beef rib (see page 174), with a double quantity of Guinness glaze so you have plenty for the burger

For the Irish burger cheese

250g (9oz) your favourite Irish cheese, diced

75ml (5 tbsp) milk

2 tsp sodium citrate

1 tsp salt

1 tbsp butter

For the charred cabbage

½ Savoy cabbage

1 tbsp rapeseed (canola) oil

Knob of butter

Salt and ground black pepper

Northern Ireland and Ireland are famous around the world for the humour, the craic, the music, the pubs, the poetry. The Guinness. I may be going for low-hanging fruit here, but if you're doing a burger inspired by the Emerald Isle, it's going to have Guinness in it.

This is a proper tower burger. You can make it more sensible by pulling the meat instead of stacking the rib whole, but where's the fun in that?

For the Irish burger cheese, place all the ingredients in a pan over a low heat and gently melt, stirring until smooth. Pour onto a tray to level out and set, and chill until sliceable – at least 1 hour, but better still overnight.

For the champ mayo, follow the instructions on page 216 and set aside.

Get your BBQ ready for 2-zone direct grilling (or a hotplate if doing a smash burger). Season the minced beef or lamb with salt and ground black pepper, or SPG, then shape into a patty – any style works for this.

Season the half cabbage with salt, pepper and the oil. Grill over direct heat for a few minutes until nicely charred. Slice thinly, then sauté in a pan with a knob of butter until soft.

Cook the burger patty on the grill as directed on page 130, then add a slice of Irish burger cheese and steam under a cloche to melt it.

To build your burger, toast your bun. Spread champ mayo over the bottom bun, then add a generous layer of the charred cabbage. Add the cheese-topped patty, then the beef rib – dip the top of the rib into a little extra champ mayo for good measure. Crown with the top bun (and, if you're feeling brave, spike the whole thing with the remaining rib bone) and enjoy with a cold pint of the black stuff.

Serves: 4

BBQ setup: Smoker

Fuel source: Lumpwood, briquettes, or all wood in an offset

Wood flavour: Oak or hickory works best

Cook time: 20–30 minutes

INGREDIENTS

680g (1lb 8oz) minced (ground) beef (50/50 chuck and brisket blend, or your own mix; just make sure it's 20–25% fat)

Salt and ground black pepper or Beefy Boys secret seasoning*

**I can't tell you what's in our secret seasoning. I'd have to kill you. Or at least try, which would be difficult because none of us are particularly fit, and none of us have any formal martial arts or assassination training. It would probably just end with us crying, out of breath and you feeling awkward. So, just go buy a tub yourself. Besides, because of the 'laws' in this country, we have to write what's in it on the back anyway.*

Smoked patties are truly unique and one of the few things in BBQ that give you that big smoky, meaty flavour hit without requiring you to stand next to a BBQ for the length of a full working day. Which is nice sometimes.

Divide the minced beef into 4 equal balls, each 170g (6oz), being careful not to overwork the meat. Gently form the balls into patties, with the emphasis on gently.

Season your patties generously with salt and pepper (or our secret seasoning if you are in the know/defeated us in combat).

Get your smoker running at around 120°C/250°F and place the patties directly on the grill grates. Smoke the patties until they reach an internal temperature of 60°C/140°F.

Take them off the grill and let them rest for a minute while you set up your BBQ for a flat-top finish. This could be a dedicated griddle, a flat-top insert, or just a heavy cast-iron pan set directly over the coals.

Once it's searing hot, place the patties on the surface to develop a bit of colour – don't overcook them here, it's literally just to get that crust and to steam. Flip them over, add your cheese and your bun lid, and spray a bit of water on the hotplate. Cover with a cloche for 30 seconds to let the steam melt everything together into burger perfection.

Check with an instant-read thermometer: your patties should be sitting at around 65°C/149°F internal temperature. (We strongly advise that for pregnant women, children or anyone immune-compromised, the patties are cooked to 75°C/167°F, just to be safe.)

Serves: 1

BBQ setup: 2-zone direct grilling (plus optional hotplate if doing smash burgers)

Fuel source: Lumpwood, briquettes, or wood burnt down to embers

Cook time: 10 minutes (plus the smoking of the beef cheek; see page 172)

INGREDIENTS

170g (6oz) minced (ground) beef

Salt and ground black pepper, or SPG (salt, pepper, garlic granules; see page 33)

2 slices of American cheese

1 semi-brioche or potato burger bun

Gherkins (optional)

1 beef dripping finished cheek (see page 172), sliced

For the pickled red chillies

600ml (2½ cups) water

120ml (½ cup) distilled white vinegar

1½ tbsp smoked rock salt

1½ tbsp sugar

3 garlic cloves

200g (7oz) red chillies, thinly sliced

For the piri-naise

225g (1 cup) mayonnaise

2 tbsp Pinho's whisky piri piri marinade (see page 206) or good shop-bought

Despite being so rich, beef cheeks make an incredible burger topping – tender, smoky and ridiculously indulgent – and they complement the right patty and toppings beautifully.

The inspiration for this burger came from all things 'cheeky', which is why we've included piri-naise and some delicious pickled red chillies. They're a great standalone pickle or perfect as a side for any BBQ dish.

For the pickled chillies, add the water, vinegar, salt, sugar and garlic cloves to a pan and bring to the boil. Place your sliced red chillies in a clean jar and pour the hot pickling liquor over them. Once cool, seal the jar. The chillies will be ready in 1 hour, but even better if left overnight. They'll keep for about a week in the fridge.

Mix the mayo and the piri piri sauce together and set aside.

Season the minced beef with salt and ground black pepper, or SPG, then shape into a patty – any style works for this: smash burgers, or go smoked if you want to double down on flavour (see page 142).

Get your BBQ ready for 2-zone direct grilling (or a hotplate if doing a smash burger). Cook the patty on the grill as directed on page 130, then add the cheese and steam under a cloche to melt it.

To assemble your burger, spread piri-naise on the base of the bun. Add your gherkins (or leave them off if you're Lee). Place your beef cheek slices on top of the cheesed patty, add your pickled chillies on top, crown with the top bun and tuck in.

INGREDIENTS

1 semi-brioche or potato burger bun

Grilled cabbage slaw (see page 194) or salad cream ranch slaw (see page 158)

170g (6oz) minced (ground) beef

Salt and ground black pepper, or SPG (salt, pepper, garlic granules; see page 33)

1 slice of American cheese (or British burger cheese; see page 132)

1 slice of Monterey Jack cheese

3 slices of smoked pork belly (see page 168)

Hot honey (see page 215)

1 burnt end (see page 170)

BBQ burgers can sometimes be seriously over the top. And this is one of those times.

The burnt end on top is completely impractical and could easily just sit in a little dish on the side. But look – when did you lose all the joy in your life? Sometimes we want a straightforward little burger, in its little bun, with its humble little gherkin and onion and sauce. But sometimes we want a burger that's going to kick in the front door, punch your cat and play a trumpet solo in your face.

This is that burger.

Toast your bun and add slaw to the bottom bun.

Season the minced beef with salt and ground black pepper, or SPG, then shape into a patty – any style works for this: smash burgers, or go smoked if you want to double down on flavour (see page 142).

Get your BBQ ready for 2-zone direct grilling (or a hotplate if doing a smash burger). Cook the patty on the grill as directed on page 130, then add the cheeses and steam under a cloche to melt it.

Place the patty on top of the slaw. Place the pork belly on the cheese and drizzle with hot honey. Place the bun lid on top, then place a burnt end on the bun lid and secure firmly with a burger stick.

Sit back, lock the door, warn the cat and prepare for a trumpet solo of full-on flavour to the face.

Serves: 2, or more as an accompaniment
BBQ setup: 2-zone direct grilling
Fuel source: Lumpwood, briquettes, or wood burnt down to embers
Cook time: Under 30 minutes

INGREDIENTS

1 large tomato
160–200g (5½–7oz) fire-roasted carrots (see page 150)
150–200g (5½–7oz) courgette (zucchini)
150–200g (5½–7oz) aubergine (eggplant)
100–150g (3½–5½oz) tenderstem broccoli
75–100g (2½–3½oz) fine green beans
60–100g (2¼–3½oz) spring onions (scallions)
Red pepper dip (see page 215)
Lemon pepper mayo (see page 216)

To season the veg
SPG (salt, pepper, garlic granules; see page 33)
Thyme leaves
Rapeseed (canola) or olive (non-virgin) oil (or you can use smoked or garlic oil)
Lemon juice

This works great on its own, or you could chuck it in the middle of a table alongside some meat or fish; it's also easy to scale up.

Tomato first. Get your tomato on before anything else. Cut it in half, season with SPG, the thyme leaves and oil. Put it high up on the BBQ so it gets a slow roast over direct heat, turning it over halfway through so it gets some good colour on both sides.

For the carrots. Follow the instructions on page 150.

Cook the courgette and aubergine. Slice your courgette and aubergine about 1cm (½ inch) thick, toss in oil, SPG and a squeeze of lemon juice. Get them over direct heat, close enough to the coals that you can't hold your hand there for longer than 2 seconds without shouting an expletive. The goal is to get a good char and cook them past the rubbery stage, especially the aubergine. Once ready, move them somewhere on the BBQ to keep warm.

Cook the rest of your veg. Toss the broccoli, beans and spring onions in oil, SPG and lemon juice. Get the veg on the grill! The broccoli will take the longest. You're looking for everything to have a nice bit of char on the outside and to be beautifully tender; as soon as you can get a fork through the veg easily, it's done.

Make the red pepper dip. Follow the instructions on page 215.

Make the lemon pepper mayo. Follow the instructions on page 216.

Assemble. Once everything is cooked, lay the veg out on a tray with the dips. Get stuck in and use the dips to give your grilled veg that extra flavour kick.

Serves: 2 as a light lunch or more as a side

BBQ setup: 2-zone direct grilling

Fuel source: Lumpwood, briquettes, or wood burnt down to embers

Cook time: 1 hour

INGREDIENTS

500g (1lb 2oz) carrots, peeled and left whole

1 tbsp salt

1 tbsp sugar

2 star anise

Knob of butter

Splash of rapeseed (canola) or olive (non-virgin) oil

Pinch of SPG (salt, pepper, garlic granules; see page 33)

A few healthy glugs of maple syrup

2 tbsp smashed-up hazelnuts (feel free to swap with any nuts)

This is the best way to cook carrots. I love this recipe so much. It works great on a regular roast, even just done in the oven as opposed to the grill, and it is always a big hit with the kids. You can kind of convince yourself it is good for them, too, because ultimately they are eating veg. It just so happens to be doused in maple syrup.

Add the carrots, salt, sugar, star anise and butter to a pan of water and bring to the boil. Turn down to a simmer and cook until you can just about stick a fork through them. Drain and allow the carrots to cool.

Set your BBQ up for direct grilling. Oil the carrots lightly and add a small amount of SPG (they will already be seasoned from the first cook).

Place the carrots on the hot grill, turning every 2–3 minutes until they take on a bit of char.

As soon as you start getting a nice bit of colour, baste with the maple syrup. Keep cooking, allowing the maple glaze to caramelize and stick to the carrots.

Once nicely glazed, remove from the grill, top with crushed hazelnuts for a bit of texture, and, if you really want, add an extra drizzle of maple syrup to the serving dish.

SMOKED BEETROOT

Serves: Flexible
BBQ setup: Smoker
Fuel source: Lumpwood or briquettes
Wood flavour: Oak
Cook time: 4–5 hours

INGREDIENTS

Beetroots (beets)

Smoked beetroot – it's a gateway veg. Once you've tried it you will be addicted. Beetroot is massively underrated. For years I thought it was just something your nan would eat out of a jar with a bit of ham. It's only now, as an adult, I realize… goddammit, my nan was ahead of her time.

Beetroot is versatile and delicious, and when smoked it transcends from nan-fridge-filler to ultimate veg that will dominate all other veg in your fridge. We recommend doing this in a big batch and keeping it in the fridge for up to five days.

A word of warning: beetroot stains and, if you eat a large amount of beetroot, it retains its colour through all stages of digestion. Not knowing this once sent me into a blind panic, thinking I was having a medical emergency.

Wash your beetroots thoroughly, removing any dirt or soil from the outside.

Get your smoker running at 120–135°C/250–275°F (you can speed this up slightly by pushing it to 150°C/302°F).

Place the beetroots in the smoker with plenty of space around them for the smoke to circulate.

Smoke for 4–5 hours, until they are tender enough to push a knife through easily.

Remove from the smoker, allow them to cool, then peel.

SMOKED BEETROOT KETCHUP

INGREDIENTS

450g (1lb) smoked beetroot/beet (see opposite), peeled and cubed (you should be left with about 300g/10½oz)

2 tbsp cider vinegar

2 tsp smoked salt

1 tsp white sugar

2 tbsp rapeseed (canola) or olive (non-virgin) oil

1 tbsp Worcestershire sauce

½ tsp cracked black pepper

Add all the ingredients to a food processor and blitz until smooth.

Adjust the thickness with a little water, if needed. Taste and check the seasoning.

Store in the fridge for up to 5 days.

FUN WITH GARLIC TWO WAYS

Who doesn't love garlic? Vampires and people on a first date. Apart from that, we all love it. Hands up who's guilty of reading a recipe that says '2 cloves of garlic' and then proceeding to use 6? Yep, us too. I think evolution gave garlic its fiddly skin because if it didn't, we'd all be throwing 20 cloves into every dish we ever made.

These two recipes aren't full dishes in themselves, but they'll give you two awesome staples for the pantry. You'll see them used throughout this book. Feel free to experiment by swapping them into any recipe that calls for garlic. They're especially good in sauces, dressings, or anywhere you'd usually use garlic raw, because smoking or confiting really takes the edge off and calms down that intense raw garlic punch.

BBQ setup: Smoker
Fuel source: Lumpwood, briquettes, or wood burnt down to embers
Wood flavour: Oak, cherry or apple all work and each gives slightly different results
Cook time: 30–45 minutes

INGREDIENTS

3–4 whole garlic bulbs, skin on (smoke as many or as few as you like, depending on the space in your smoker)

SMOKED GARLIC

Get your smoker running at a steady 120°C/250°F.

Place the garlic on the smoker and cook for 30–45 minutes, until the bulbs have turned a rich brown, smoky colour and feel soft and squidgy.

Let cool before use. Keeps in the fridge for 4–5 days.

BBQ setup: 2-zone for direct grilling (to be honest, you can also do this inside on the stovetop with less chance of messing up the temperatures)

Fuel source: Lumpwood, briquettes, or wood burnt down to embers

Cook time: 1 hour

INGREDIENTS

20 garlic cloves

Sprinkle of rock salt

150g (5½oz) beef fat (or enough to cover the garlic)

3 sprigs of rosemary

Peel the garlic and sprinkle with a little rock salt.

Place the beef fat into a saucepan and melt it down. Add the garlic and rosemary to the beef fat, making sure the garlic is fully submerged.

Cook over a super-low heat for around 1 hour until the garlic is soft and jammy. Watch out, you don't want to burn the garlic or it will go bitter. A smidge of light brown is fine, but don't take it any further. Low and slow is the key.

Once ready, remove the garlic from the fat and place it in a small container. Refrigerate. If you're not using it within 1–2 days, pour a neutral oil over the top to seal and keep it fresh (if you use the beef dripping itself, it will go rock solid).

Result: Voilà, two amazing ingredients for the price of one – delicious beef fat confit garlic, and garlic-and-rosemary-infused beef fat. Both will keep refrigerated for up to 5 days.

Serves: 2–3 as a meal, or loads of people as a side

BBQ setup: Direct grilling and BBQ roasting

Fuel source: Lumpwood, briquettes, or wood burnt down to embers

Cook time: 50 minutes

INGREDIENTS

1 large cauliflower

1 small head of broccoli

Rapeseed (canola) or olive (non-virgin) oil, for coating

75g (⅓ cup) butter

75g (½ cup plus 1 tbsp) plain (all-purpose) flour

600ml (2½ cups) milk

250g (9oz) Cheddar, grated

2 slices of American cheese

2 tsp English mustard

2 tbsp freshly grated Parmesan

Salt and ground black pepper

Cauliflower cheese – the unsung hero of the Sunday roast. It's rich, cheesy and comforting like Daniel O'Donnell. This version picks up smoky flavour from the BBQ and a bit of colour on the florets before being finished off in a roasting zone. It's great alongside a roast, but honestly, it holds its own with just a bit of green salad and a cold beer.

Prep and grill. Set your BBQ up for direct grilling. Break the cauliflower and broccoli into large florets, toss them in a little oil and season with salt and pepper.

Grill the florets directly over the heat for a few minutes until they start to take on a bit of colour. You're not trying to cook them through here, just adding some smoky flavour and char. Transfer the charred florets to a deep baking dish.

Make the cheese sauce. Melt the butter in a saucepan over a medium heat. Add the flour and stir to make a roux. Cook it out for a couple of minutes, then slowly add the milk, while whisking constantly, to make a smooth béchamel.

Add the Cheddar, American cheese and mustard, stir until the cheese has fully melted, then season to taste with salt and pepper.

Pour the sauce over the cauliflower and broccoli, then sprinkle the Parmesan over the top.

BBQ roast. Set your BBQ for roasting or fire up a wood-fired oven at around 180–200°C/350–400°F. Place the dish inside and cook for 30–35 minutes, until the cauliflower is tender and the top is golden, bubbling and caramelized.

Serve straight from the dish while it's still molten and gooey.

Serves: 8 as a side
BBQ setup: Direct grilling
Fuel source: Lumpwood, briquettes, or wood burnt down to embers
Cook time: 20 minutes

INGREDIENTS

For the slaw

1 white cabbage, quartered
½ red cabbage, quartered
Rapeseed (canola) oil, for coating the cabbage
3 large carrots, grated
½ celeriac (celery root), peeled and grated
Salt and ground black pepper

For the salad cream ranch dressing

1 garlic clove, chopped and crushed with a little rock salt
1 tbsp chopped dill
2 tbsp chopped chives
2 tbsp grated Parmesan
170g (¾ cup) mayonnaise
170g (¾ cup) salad cream

The British are a docile lot, pretty much taking in our stride whatever madcap scheme our revolving door of prime ministers fancies, but I am old enough to remember the Salad Cream Riots of 1999, when rumours spread that manufacturers were considering discontinuing it. For anyone out there whose back doesn't hurt, you might not realize that in the 1980s salad cream was everywhere. We could only dare to dream of mayonnaise. Salad cream reigned supreme. I didn't see real mayo until I was nearly a man.

Such over salad-creamification meant it fell out of favour, leading to the brief moment where manufacturers flirted with taking it off the shelves. But to avoid a complete national breakdown into a Mad Max-style civilization, the government reinstated it; then we as the general public have happily continued to ignore it to this day.

But not us. We're bringing it back with our Salad Cream Ranch Slaw. Grilling your cabbages really helps bring a bit of fire and flavour to your slaw, too!

Set up your BBQ for direct grilling.

Rub all the cabbage quarters with oil and season with salt and pepper. Place directly on the grill and cook for about 5 minutes, then turn and cook for a few more minutes until you've built up a nice char. Remove and allow to cool completely.

Combine all the ranch dressing ingredients in a bowl and set aside to let the flavours develop.

To build the slaw, finely slice the grilled cabbage and combine with the grated carrots and celeriac. Mix everything together with the dressing and season to taste.

WES
Disney World
TRANS
ATLA

DALLAS
NTIC
BBQ
Franklin
BARB

To be clear, we have no problem with American BBQ. It's the genesis of the majority of things written in this book, and if it wasn't for American burgers and BBQ we wouldn't be doing what we are today. American BBQ is a craft, it's an art. You need decades working a pit before you would even dream of calling yourself a pitmaster. It's this commitment to the art and craft that has made American-style BBQ so exciting and enticing to us Brits. It's the reason the majority of us in the UK who take BBQ seriously do what we do.

The problem is, the majority of American-style BBQ doesn't work in the UK.

Picture us hapless Brits getting super excited after reading an American BBQ book. We are dreaming of the incredible low-and-slow meats we've read about. We head to our butcher to get an amazing slab of thick, juicy pork ribs. We purchase our ribs, we head home, we unwrap them... and we see they are nothing like the ones in the cookbooks. These ribs are thin, the wrong size, bones showing everywhere. We ignore it, determined to make some amazing ribs. We rub them up, chuck them on the BBQ, follow the recipe and techniques to the letter and end up with a dried-up rack of 80% bones and slivers of dried-out meat in between. At best it's dry, at worst it's pork jerky. Nightmarish stuff.

Even worse is fantasizing about some mouth-watering, melt-in-the-mouth brisket just like you've read about at Franklin's. You follow the recipe, excitement builds, you big your BBQ skills up to your friends and family. You spend 14 hours watching your BBQ temp gauge like a hawk, you fight through poor weather and sleep deprivation to cook the most famous mouthful in BBQ. You invite your friends and family, everyone's waiting

eagerly to try the holy grail of the pit. You take your brisket out from resting, you unwrap it, it looks good on the outside, excitement builds. You slice it, expecting to see fountains of brisket juice pouring like a waterfall onto the chopping board. You look at your slice of brisket... it's dry. You hope it tastes better than it looks. You followed the recipe exactly, it's got to be perfect, right?

You try it. Your friends try it. They all nod as they chew. They don't immediately respond. 'The flavour's nice.' 'You can taste the smoke.' 'It's a touch dry,' someone dares to mention. You know it's dry. They know it's dry. No one else says anything. They're still chewing.

The next day you feel dejected. You start thinking, what's all the fuss about brisket? It's just like a smoky version of your nan's overcooked roast beef. You go online, you start telling people brisket is overrated. You just can't fathom what the fuss is about.

Now, just to be clear, anyone who ever says brisket is overrated has never had a good one. A perfectly cooked brisket is a near spiritual experience. How could it be that yours never reached such heights?

What did you do wrong? The truth is, you've been done dirty. You were set up to fail from the start. The bitter pill to swallow is that as amazing as British meat is, some of it just isn't suited to traditional American BBQ.

Why, though? Different reasons for different cuts. The two standouts when trying to replicate the Americans are the two examples above: ribs and brisket.

Generally, British pork ribs are awful. Firstly, our pigs aren't quite as big as their cousins over the pond. Secondly, British butchers and consumers love pork belly. The belly sits on top of the rib cage. Our consumers and butchers in the UK prize the belly, so when butchering the pig they go as tight to the ribs as possible. In America it's the other way round, with butchers choosing to cut the pork ribs with more meat on top. You can get around this in the UK by getting friendly with your butcher, something we advise everyone to do. A friend in need is a friend indeed, but a friend at the butchers is better. Get them a Christmas card, take them out for a nice dinner, compliment them, buy them flowers. Before you know it, they'll be slinging you the odd free bit of fillet and open to leaving more meat on the pork ribs for you; downside, they might think you are flirting, so be careful.

Brisket is a whole other matter. The primary difference between British and American beef is the way it's fed. The vast majority of UK beef is predominately grass-fed. American beef is primarily grain- or soy-fed. Think of it like the difference between eating a diet of salad or a diet of junk food. Grass-fed cows are leaner but packed full of flavour from their diet. Grain-fed cows have more marbling, making them more tender than their British counterparts. It's this extra marbling that makes American briskets so incredibly well suited to low-and-slow BBQ, and it's the lack of marbling in British briskets that makes them incredibly difficult to cook low and slow without them drying out.

The easiest solution is to just buy a grain-fed brisket. But there's an environmental impact with that as well. Grain-fed beef is far worse for the environment than grass-fed, and generally any grain-fed beef you buy will have been flown halfway across the world before landing on your smoker in the UK. That's not really sustainable, and it's something we should think seriously about when we already have such amazing meat here in the UK.

Our goal with this section of the book is to take huge inspiration from the pitmasters in the US and give it a British spin. We want to use meats and cuts that are the best of British and that actually work for low-and-slow BBQ, while also taking ingredients that are staples in the UK and giving them a transatlantic BBQ twist.

THE BEEFY BBQ

BBQ was always something we wanted to offer at The Beefy Boys. It's ingrained in us from our early days at BBQ competitions, before we decided to specialize in steamy meat patties between buns.

To do BBQ well for the public, you need a pitmaster. Someone dedicated to the art and craft of BBQ. Someone who lives and breathes it, and welcomes 12–14-hour days next to a firebox – stoking, spritzing, wrapping – treating those fine low-and-slow cuts of meat with the time and respect they deserve.

We were lucky enough to hear about another lad in Hereford doing amazing things with meat and smoke. We sought him out, tried his food, and in one bite we knew we'd found someone who *got it, got the food, got the culture*. Someone knocking out BBQ in our hometown that was just as good as what we'd tried in the States.

That man was **Ashley Tunley**, and his pop-up **Big Smoke BBQ**.

We met up with Ash and realized pretty quickly he had the skills, the drive, and the passion. So we asked him if he'd like to come and be The Beefy Boys' resident pitmaster. Since then, he's been banging out world-class BBQ every week at our Hereford site.

Ash's journey into BBQ is very similar to ours – a backyard BBQer who took his hobby and turned it into a career. There may even be a few of you reading this now who've thought about making the jump from the daily grind to the nightly smoke, and it's worth hearing Ash's story in his own words.

My introduction to the world of craft BBQ started purely by accident. In 2020, during the pandemic, I wanted to buy a cheap charcoal grill to badly cook sausages and burgers on. What I ended up buying for less than £100 was a cheap offset smoker.

With absolutely no idea how to use it or what it did, I turned to Google and YouTube and found myself going deeper and deeper down the rabbit hole of smoked BBQ. I spent the next few months watching several big YouTubers and realized pretty quickly that smoking a rack of ribs in the garden, sipping on a nice cold beer or three, and smoking a cigar, was just about the greatest way to spend a spare afternoon.

It meant I was 'busy' for hours. I became obsessed with the process of running a fire yourself, cooking meat low and slow, and trying to replicate what I saw on social media.

I did my first pop-up in August 2021, alongside takeaway collections from home once a month, and it became successful very quickly. From 2023 onwards I was doing pop-up events at pubs, breweries and other venues most weekends, right up until the end of 2024.

Murf from The Beefy Boys came along to one of my pop-ups in 2024 and really enjoyed the food. Dan, one of the other co-owners, came to the next one and said the same. Fast-forward to 2025 and I sat down with Murf to work on a BBQ project that's gone from strength to strength called The Beefy BBQ, where we offer amazing craft BBQ every week.

What started as a total mistake – ordering the wrong BBQ – has turned into a really successful venture, and is now my full-time job.

Crazy.

Serves: 4–8

BBQ setup: Smoker

Fuel source: Lumpwood, briquettes, or all wood in an offset

Wood flavour: Oak, apple, cherry

Cook time: 6–8 hours

INGREDIENTS

4–5kg (8¾–11lb) rind-off pork belly

Cracked black pepper

SPG (salt, pepper, garlic granules; see page 33), your favourite rub, or regular salt

Spritz made of 50/50 water and cider vinegar

Pork belly is such a great cut to BBQ, especially when you are learning. It is really hard to dry a pork belly out, and in BBQ terms an 8-hour cook is not actually that long. (Yes, that might sound like ages, but to a pitmaster 8 hours is only one step up from boiling an egg. It is part-time smoking!) Learning how to BBQ a pork belly also unlocks the world of burnt ends, so it is a double whammy to learn and master this recipe!

Get your pork belly from the butcher and make sure you ask for the rind off. Keep the rind, though, because you can turn it into crackling or pork scratchings.

Take the pork belly and cut it into 4 pieces. You will notice that some parts are much thicker than others, and that difference in thickness has a big impact on cooking times; when you break the belly down into pieces, aim to keep them as even in thickness as possible. Remove any scraggly or flaky bits of meat still attached, and gently round off any hard edges or points. Always be mindful of how the smoke will travel over the belly! Think sleek and smooth like a sports car.

Once your belly pieces are nice and aerodynamic, season them up. Coarse black pepper first plus either SPG, your favourite BBQ rub, or just plain salt. Remember that pork belly is only seasoned on the outside, so it can take a good amount of seasoning.

Get the pit running at 135°C/275°F with some nice rolling smoke. Place the belly pieces fat-side up and smoke for 4 hours before lifting the lid to check colour and progress. Spritz the pieces and move any around that are cooking too quickly or too slowly. Close the lid again and keep smoking until they reach an internal temperature of 82–88°C/180–190°F. Be careful not to take them too close to 96°C/205°F, or they will fall apart and turn into pulled pork.

Once your pork pieces have rested for a few minutes, slice them up and enjoy that delicious rendered fat and beautiful smoky pork.

Serves: 4–8

BBQ setup: Smoker

Fuel source: Lumpwood, briquettes, or all wood in an offset

Wood flavour: Oak, apple, cherry

Cook time: 6–8 hours, plus optional overnight chilling

INGREDIENTS

Smoked pork belly (see page 168)

Hot honey (see page 215), or glaze of your choice

Burnt ends are the guilty pleasure of BBQ. Whenever I come home from working a BBQ night, I always bring a takeaway box of leftover meat. My wife will literally fight a man to the death (that man being me) to get those burnt ends. They never last longer than a minute or two after I walk through the door, and I get it. Rich, tender, and open to be dressed with a million different sauce combos, they are the pick-and-mix of BBQ.

This recipe lays out the basic process of cooking burnt ends. The exciting part is the glazes. See pages 214–217 for sauce ideas and ways to finish your burnt ends.

There are two ways to make burnt ends, and both start with the pork belly recipe on page 168. The 2-day method below can be really handy if you are having guests round and you don't want to be glued to a BBQ for 8 hours of the day.

For the hot honey, follow the instructions on page 215, or use a glaze of your choice.

OPTION 1 — ALL IN ONE DAY

Follow the pork belly recipe on page 168 but remove the pieces when they hit 75°C/167°F.

Let them cool for 10–20 minutes, then cut into 2–2.5cm (¾–1 inch) cubes.

Place the cubes in a foil tray, pour over your hot honey or chosen glaze and return them to the smoker at 135°C/275°F.

Cook until they reach an internal temperature of around 90°C/194°F, glazing again during the cook if you fancy.

Take them out, rest them for a minute or two, and dive in, glazed with hot honey or your chosen glaze.

OPTION 2 — SPLIT OVER TWO DAYS

Follow the pork belly recipe on page 168 but take the pieces to 80–85°C/176–185°F.

Remove from the smoker and chill to below 10°C/50°F within 90 minutes. (You can help this along by placing your container on top of a bed of ice and keeping the pork belly all in one layer and not crowded together.)

Keep the pieces in the fridge overnight.

The next day, cube into 2–2.5cm (¾–1 inch) cubes.

Place in a foil tray, add your hot honey or chosen glaze, and smoke at 135°C/275°F until the burnt ends hit 90°C/194°F.

Rest briefly, then glaze with more hot honey or your chosen glaze.

Serves: 1–2

BBQ setup: Smoker

Fuel source: Lumpwood, briquettes, or all wood in an offset

Wood flavour: Oak, cherry, pecan all work beautifully (oak is the classic pairing)

Cook time: 8 hours

INGREDIENTS

300–400g (10½–14oz) beef cheeks

Cracked black pepper

SPG (salt, pepper, garlic granules; see page 33), your favourite rub, or regular salt

Enough beef dripping to fully submerge the cheeks

TOP TIP

You can use these beef cheeks for our cheeky boy burger recipe on page 144, or some beef cheek tacos using our beef fat taco shell recipe (pages 210–211).

Think of beef cheeks like mini briskets: cheaper, easier to cook and, for my money, even better than brisket when done right.

Prep. Beef cheeks don't need a ton of trimming. Just remove any silver skin, hard lumps of fat, or scraggly bits dangling off. Don't stress too much, they'll be confited in beef dripping later, so anything gnarly will soften up in the cook.

Season with a generous hit of coarse black pepper; you can go a bit heavier here since some will be lost in the confit stage. Follow this with either SPG, your favourite rub or, just plain salt.

Smoke. Set your smoker steady at 135°C/275°F with your chosen wood. Bold flavours are going to work really well with something as incredibly rich as a beef cheek.

Place the cheeks on the pit and smoke at 135°C for about 4 hours before checking. You're aiming for a deep, dark bark. Check the internal temperature; you want to be hitting around 75°C/167°F. If they're not quite there, you could give them a light spritz – a vinegar, mustard or hot sauce spritz would be best. Keep smoking until you hit that 75°C/167°F sweet spot. This can take anywhere from 4 to 6 hours from the start of the cook, depending on your smoker and the cheeks themselves.

Confit. Once the cheeks are at 75°C/167°F, it's time for the confit stage. Melt down your beef dripping in an oven tray until it's warm and liquid, then submerge the cheeks fully. Place back in the smoker for another 2 hours at 135°C/275°F until the internal temperature hits 96°C/205°F, then remove and leave to rest for a few minutes.

This confit stage doesn't need to be smoked, so feel free to move them into the oven or onto the stovetop if you want to save fuel and/or free up smoker space. While 135°C/275°F is the optimum temperature, you can go a bit higher than that if needed. The beef dripping will help protect the cheeks. But be careful not to go too high; you are after a confit not a deep-fry!

Serve. Once the cheeks have rested, slice them up and dive into easily one of the best bites in all of British BBQ.

Serves: 2–4

BBQ setup: Smoker

Fuel source: Lumpwood, briquettes, or all wood in an offset

Wood flavour: Oak, pecan, hickory or mesquite

Cook time: 8 hours

INGREDIENTS

For the ribs

1 x 3-bone rack of Jacob's ladder beef ribs

1 tbsp English mustard

2 tsp coarsely ground black pepper

2 tbsp your favourite BBQ rub or a 50/50 mix of salt and garlic granules

Guinness glaze (see page 217)

80ml (⅓ cup) beef tallow or dripping

For the spritz

80ml (⅓ cup) malt vinegar

80ml (⅓ cup) Worcestershire sauce

80ml (⅓ cup) water

1 tsp English mustard

This is our kind of BBQ – not just low and slow, but low and slow with zero fuss. No trimming, no fancy prep, just get the ribs on the smoker, cook them up, and enjoy.

Set up your smoker. Get your BBQ running steady at 120°C/250°F with a few chunks of oak or your chosen wood.

Prep the ribs. Jacob's ladder ribs rarely need trimming, but if there are any scraggly bits, tidy them up. Rub the ribs all over with the mustard, season with the black pepper, then add your rub or salt mix. Place the ribs on the smoker, close the lid and smoke for 3 hours.

Spritz time. Make your spritz by whisking all the ingredients together and pouring into a spray bottle. After 3 hours, lift the lid and check on the ribs. If the colour and bark are starting to look good, spritz them all over and close the lid again.

Midway check. After another 2 hours, open up and spritz again. You can bump the smoker up to 150°C/300°F now if you want to speed things along.

Make the Guinness glaze. While the ribs are cooking, follow the instructions on page 217.

Glaze and finish. Around the 6-hour mark, the ribs should be pushing into the mid 80s (temperature, not the decade; around 185°F). Brush on a generous layer of the Guinness glaze and close the lid again. Keep checking every 30–40 minutes until the ribs hit 93–94°C/199–201°F internal temperature.

Once they reach that point, take them off the heat, then set aside. The carryover heat will take them to 96°C/205°F.

Rest like a champion. Melt your beef tallow in a pan. Lay out some butcher's paper or foil, place the ribs in the middle, pour the tallow over the top and wrap them up tightly. Let them rest for around 45 minutes until the internal temperature drops to about 65°C/149°F. That's your sweet spot: perfect, juicy, tender beef ribs ready to eat.

Slice them up, use any leftover glaze as a dip, and serve.

Serves: 4–6

BBQ setup: Smoker

Fuel source: Lumpwood, briquettes, or all wood in an offset

Wood flavour: Oak, pecan, hickory or mesquite

Cook time: 12 hours

INGREDIENTS

1 beef shank, French trimmed

Garlic granules or your favourite BBQ rub

4 tbsp beef dripping

Salt and coarsely ground black pepper

For the mac and cheese

1kg (2lb 4oz) dried macaroni

375ml (1½ cups) milk

4 tsp sodium citrate

1kg (2lb 4oz) strong Cheddar

500g (1lb 2oz) cheese of your choice (Double Gloucester, Gruyère, Stilton, Stinking Bishop… go nuts)

2 tbsp butter

1 tsp English mustard

1 tbsp truffle oil

2 tsp salt

A BBQ feast fit for the god of thunder. This is a French-trimmed beef shank – a real showstopper and perfect for sharing. Mac and cheese is always a winner with BBQ, and who doesn't like mac and cheese?

Season the Thor's hammer all over with black pepper followed by salt and garlic granules, or your favourite BBQ rub.

Set your BBQ up between 120°C/250°F and 150°C/300°F. Smoke the shank for 9 hours, or until it reaches an internal temperature of around 80°C/176°F. Smother it in beef dripping, wrap in foil or butcher's paper, then return it to the BBQ and continue cooking until it reaches 96°C/205°F internal temperature.

Unwrap the beef. It was happily rest submerged in warm beef dripping at around 65°C/149°F until ready to serve.

For the mac and cheese, cook the macaroni in a pan of salted boiling water until al dente. Drain and run cold water over it to stop it cooking and to cool it down.

Add the milk and sodium citrate to a large pan over a low heat, stirring until dissolved. Grate or cube all the cheese and add it to the milk mixture, stirring until fully melted. Add the butter, mustard, truffle oil and salt. Taste and adjust the seasoning.

Add the drained pasta to the sauce and stir well, then decant into a serving bowl.

Pull your Thor's hammer apart and shred the meat straight into the mac and cheese. Serve with pickles and BBQ sauce. Praise Odin!

Serves: 1–2

BBQ setup: Smoker

Fuel source: Lumpwood, briquettes, or all wood in an offset

Wood flavour: Oak, cherry or apple

Cook time: 8 hours

INGREDIENTS

1 rack of lamb ribs (ask your butcher for lamb breast on the bone)

Garlic granules or your favourite BBQ rub

Salt and coarsely ground black pepper

For the marmalade BBQ glaze

340g (1 cup) marmalade

170g (½ cup) honey

80ml (⅓ cup) orange juice

80g (⅓ cup) tomato ketchup

2 tsp salt

½ tsp cayenne pepper

2 tbsp apple cider vinegar

For the spritz

120ml (½ cup) water

120ml (½ cup) red wine vinegar

3 tbsp Worcestershire sauce

Lamb ribs are naughty. There is just something glorious about rendered lamb fat, and to cut through that richness we have taken a leaf out of national treasure Paddington's book and paired the ribs with an awesome marmalade-based BBQ sauce. It goes ridiculously well with lamb, but you can use this as a regular BBQ sauce for almost everything.

To make the marmalade BBQ glaze, add all the ingredients to a saucepan and place over a medium heat until combined. Let it bubble for a couple of minutes, stirring, then set aside.

Season your lamb ribs with black pepper followed by salt and garlic granules, or your favourite BBQ rub.

Get your smoker running at 120°C/250°F and mix up your spritz ingredients. Place the ribs on the smoker and cook for around 6 hours, spritzing them every 2 hours.

Continue to cook for another 2 hours, until the ribs reach an internal temperature of around 96°C/205°F and the fat is nicely rendered. You should be able to wiggle the bones with very little resistance.

Brush the ribs generously with the marmalade glaze. Give the glaze a few minutes on the ribs to set, then wrap them and keep them warm until ready to serve, ideally alongside a talking bear in a coat.

Serves: 2

BBQ setup: Smoker

Fuel source: Lumpwood, briquettes, or all wood in an offset

Wood flavour: Oak, cherry or pecan

Cook time: 8 hours

INGREDIENTS

1 whole oxtail (900g–1.2kg/ 2–2lb 10oz), in sections

Garlic granules or your favourite BBQ rub

Enough beef dripping to fully submerge the oxtail

Salt and coarsely ground black pepper

We should all be eating more oxtail. It is like beef if you turned it up to 11. It is beef if it was directed by Zack Snyder. It is beef portrayed by Daniel Day-Lewis. What I am trying to say is, it is very beefy.

Ridiculously rich and tender, when it is slow-smoked then confited in beef dripping it becomes an esoteric journey into beef. The great news is that, unlike almost every other BBQ cut, it is relatively cheap. So get down to your butcher, get some oxtail, and get it on your smoker.

Season up the oxtail sections. Pepper first, then salt and garlic granules or your chosen rub.

Get your smoker running at 120°C/250°F. Place the oxtail on the smoker and cook for around 6 hours, or until the meat reaches about 80°C/176°F internal temperature.

Take the oxtail off the smoker and place it in a pot. Submerge it completely in beef dripping, return the pot to the smoker for about 2 hours and continue to cook until the oxtail reaches 96°C/205°F internal temperature. The meat should be fall-apart tender.

Serve with pickles to cut through all that glorious beef richness.

MAPLE BRINED TURKEY BREAST

Serves: 4–8

BBQ setup: Smoker

Fuel source: Lumpwood, briquettes, or all wood in an offset

Wood flavour: Oak, hickory, apple or cherry

Cook time: 2–3 hours, plus 48 hours brining

INGREDIENTS

2 turkey breasts (1.25–1.5kg/ 2lb 12oz–3lb 5oz each)
2 tbsp cracked black pepper
Your favourite BBQ rub
2 good knobs of butter

For the brine
65g (2½oz) smoked salt
325g (1 cup) maple syrup
1 tsp MSG (optional)
1.4 litres (6 cups) water

When it's cooked right, smoked turkey is honestly one of the best bites of BBQ you can get. People often worry about turkey being dry, but that's not something to lose sleep over when you cook it like this. It's juicy, smoky and somehow still light. The secret is a long brine and a short cook, for a guaranteed crowd-pleaser.

Make the brine. In a large pan over a medium heat, combine all the brine ingredients. Stir until everything is dissolved and mixed through. Let the brine cool completely, then pop it in the fridge while you prep the turkey.

Prep the turkey. Trim your turkey breasts. Remove the skin – underneath you'll find a thin second layer of skin; try to peel that off too if you can (don't worry if you don't get it all). Cut away any scraggly or stray edges so the breasts are nice and streamlined.

Place the turkey in a large container and pour over the chilled brine. Make sure the meat is fully submerged; if it's floating, weight it down with something. Cover and refrigerate for 48 hours.

Smoke the turkey. On the day of the cook, set up your smoker at 135°C/275°F with a few chunks of your chosen wood (we like oak).

Take the turkey out of the brine, pat it completely dry and give it a light coating of cracked black pepper. This gives the smoke something to stick to. Follow up with a light dusting of your favourite BBQ rub. It's already brined, so it doesn't need too much seasoning.

Place the turkey breasts on the smoker and cook for 2–3 hours, or until the internal temperature hits 65°C/149°F.

Rest and serve. Remove the turkey from the smoker, rest it for 5 minutes, then wrap it in foil or butcher's paper with the butter. Let it rest for another 15 minutes so it can bask in all that buttery goodness.

Carve into beautiful slices and serve on its own or piled high in a bun with BBQ sauce and slaw. If you want to go all out, you can dip each slice in clarified butter before serving. It's also great in sandwiches the next day, if there's any left, which there probably won't be.

Serves: 4–8

BBQ setup: Smoker

Fuel source: Lumpwood, briquettes, or all wood in an offset

Wood flavour: Oak, hickory, apple or cherry

Cook time: 2–2½ hours, plus optional overnight dry brining

INGREDIENTS

20 chicken drumsticks

BBQ sauce glaze (see page 217) or golden chipotle syrup (see page 216)

For the chicken BBQ rub (or use your favourite rub)

1 tbsp salt

1 tsp chicken powder

1 tbsp garlic granules

½ tbsp smoked paprika

½ tbsp ground black pepper

Chicken drumsticks have always been a staple of the Great British BBQ. They usually came in two varieties: black, crispy and seemingly forged in the fires of hell, looking like Anakin Skywalker after a fight on Mustafar; or insipid, slightly pink and cooked under a 70-watt light bulb.

Very rarely did you get a great one. But trimming them properly and smoking them like this gives you an awesome bite of chicken every time. The lollipop (popsicle) trimming is optional. It looks great, but feel free to skip it if you want to chow down on the whole leg. Almost any glaze will work with these (see page 217), but we thoroughly recommend the golden chipotle syrup or straight-up BBQ sauce glaze.

Mix the rub ingredients together in a bowl.

Prep the chicken by taking a sharp knife and cutting just past one-third of the way down each drumstick. Trim away all the meat, skin and tendons to leave a clean bone showing. Dust the chicken all over with your rub and leave for at least 1 hour, or ideally overnight in the fridge.

Fire up your smoker and get it running at around 150°C/300°F with your chosen wood. Place the chicken on the smoker (you may want to wrap the ends of the bones in a little foil to stop them burning) and smoke for about 1½ hours.

Meanwhile, get the glaze ready. If using BBQ sauce glaze, follow the instructions on page 217.

Or, to make the golden chipotle syrup, follow the instructions on page 216.

Once the chicken lollipops have smoked, lift the smoker lid and glaze the chicken generously with either the BBQ sauce or chipotle syrup. Close the lid, and keep glazing every 10 minutes until the chicken hits an internal temperature of 80°C/176°F.

Pile them up on a plate and tuck in.

Serves: 6–8

BBQ setup: Smoker

Fuel source: Lumpwood, briquettes, or all wood in an offset

Wood flavour: Oak, pecan, hickory or mesquite

Cook time: 6–12 hours depending on method, plus optional overnight dry brining

As we touched on earlier, brisket is the king of American BBQ. Anyone who says brisket is overrated just hasn't had a good one. We had never had a truly great one until we went to the States.

The reason is simple. British grass-fed brisket cooks completely differently to American grain-fed brisket because the marbling is totally different. Grain-fed beef is fattier and well protected through the cook, with plenty of intramuscular fat to render and keep it juicy. British grass-fed beef is leaner and behaves differently during a long smoke.

So if we are sticking with our Great British BBQ concept we have two choices. One: get a more well-marbled British brisket such as British wagyu. Two: change how we cook a standard British brisket. We are not known for decisiveness at The Beefy Boys, so we have decided to give you both.

1 full packer British brisket

Coarsely ground black pepper

Salt and garlic granules or your favourite BBQ rub

Spritz made of 50/50 water and Worcestershire sauce

480ml (2 cups) beef dripping

Trim your brisket by removing any excess fat, bits that stick out or might burn or impede the cook. Trimming a brisket is about making it as aerodynamic as possible. Season with black pepper first followed by salt and garlic, or your rub, and leave overnight to dry.

On the day of the cook, get your smoker running between 150 and 165°C/ 300 and 330°F. You want a slightly dirtier smoke at the start to help build bark. Put the brisket on the smoker and cook for 3 hours, spritzing occasionally.

After 3 hours, take it off and lay out a sheet of foil or butcher's paper. Brush the foil or paper with the beef dripping and wrap your brisket tightly. Put it back on the smoker for another hour.

Start probing. You want the brisket to hit 93°C/200°F internal temperature and feel like butter when probed. Some briskets may need slightly higher heat to get there.

Once tender, take it off the smoker and unwrap it. Let it vent so the temperature drops (if you leave it wrapped it will continue cooking and may dry out). Let it cool to around 65°C/149°F. You can now rewrap and keep it warm until ready to eat, or slice and serve straight away.

INGREDIENTS

1 full packer British Wagyu brisket
Coarsely ground black pepper
Salt and garlic granules, or your favourite BBQ rub
480ml (2 cups) beef tallow

Trim your brisket following the instructions opposite. Season the underside heavily with coarse black pepper, then the sides, then the top. Finish the top with salt and garlic granules, or your rub.

Leave the brisket uncovered in the fridge overnight to dry brine and help the bark develop. If cooking straight away that is still fine.

Put the brisket on the smoker with the point end facing the fire. Start with a smoky fire when the smoker is around 80°C/176°F rising to 110°C/230°F. You want plenty of smoke early on to build flavour and bark. Smoke at 110°C/230°F for the first 2 hours.

After 2 hours, increase the smoker to 120–125°C/250–257°F and hold it there for the next 6 hours. After around 6 hours, loosely cover the ends of the brisket with foil to protect them. Flip the brisket so the point faces away from the fire.

Run the smoker at 120–135°C/250–275°F to help push through the stall (see page 26). When the brisket reaches around 80°C/176°F internal temperature, or when the surface looks dry with no beads of moisture, make a foil boat, rub the inside with the beef tallow, and sit the brisket inside so the top can continue developing bark.

Put the brisket back on the smoker and flip it again so the point is towards the fire. Increase your smoker to 135–150°C/275–300°F to finish the cook. Once wrapped, the brisket no longer needs protection from heat. Start checking tenderness once the internal temperature hits 93°C/200°F. A brisket is usually done between 94 and 98°C/201 and 208°F, depending on the cut. Probe the middle of the flat. When it slides in like butter, the brisket is done.

Lift it off and let it cool until it drops to around 68–70°C/154–158°F. Wrap fully in foil with a little beef tallow, then wrap it in cling film (plastic wrap). Hold in a warmer if you can. Ideally rest it overnight at 65°C/149°F.

If you are eating straight away, do not slice until the brisket has cooled to around 65°C/149°F.

LOW AND SLOW - TIPS, TRICKS

Writing a BBQ recipe is hard. On paper it says '120°C (250°F) for 6 hours', but the reality of achieving that can be far from simple. Getting good at smoking meat comes down to one thing: practice. The more you do it, the more you learn, the better you get. What follows are the tips we wish we'd known when we started.

SEASONING - ORDER MATTERS

Always apply coarse seasoning first. Pepper before finer rubs. If you go in with a fine rub first, the pepper won't stick and you'll be dropping cracked peppercorns everywhere.

SMOKE - WHAT YOU'RE ACTUALLY TRYING TO DO

Creating smoke on a BBQ can be done in a few ways. Stick burners or offset smokers work by starting with a good bed of coals or embers, then feeding the fire with fresh wood. Most other BBQ setups use briquettes or lumpwood as the main heat source, with wood chunks or chips added for smoke.

You don't need to soak your wood. Soaked wood doesn't make more smoke, it just makes steam. Dry wood goes straight on the coals and burns cleanly.

Your goal with smoke is flavour and bark. But here's the important bit: not all smoke is the same.

GOOD SMOKE VS DIRTY SMOKE

Good smoke is thin, light, and often has a faint blue tinge. Dirty smoke is thick, white, and cloudy.

Conventional BBQ wisdom says you should only ever cook with clean smoke. That's mostly true. Dirty smoke can overpower food and leave it bitter and acrid if you overdo it. But here's the secret: the best BBQ has a little bit of dirty smoke.

When we start smoking a piece of meat, especially a big cut, we'll often hit it with 20–30 minutes of dirtier smoke at the beginning. This helps build colour and bark early on. After that, we switch to clean smoke for the rest of the cook. Use dirty smoke like seasoning. A little goes a long way.

Good smoke comes from a hot, well-ventilated fire. Dirty smoke happens when the fire isn't quite hot enough, airflow is restricted, or too much fuel is added at once. Too much dirty smoke will ruin an expensive cut very quickly.

MANAGING THE FIRE (THIS IS THE ACTUAL JOB)

A good way to think about low-and-slow BBQ is this: you're not cooking meat, you're managing a fire.

You want it steady and controlled, without wild flare-ups or massive temperature swings. Patience is everything.

Your vents are your tools. Think of the bottom vent as the accelerator and the top vent as the brake. The bottom feeds oxygen to the fire. The top controls how hard the BBQ pulls air through itself.

Learning how these two work together is the key to banging BBQ.

WOOD IS AN INGREDIENT

Think of wood like seasoning. Different woods bring different flavours.

OAK Strong, classic, versatile. Works with almost everything.

APPLE & PEAR Light, subtle, fruity. Perfect for pork, chicken, game.

CHERRY Big colour, big flavour. Sits between oak and fruit woods.

ALDER, BEECH, BIRCH Mild, sweet, nutty. Great with poultry, pork, fish.

ASH & HAZEL More robust than fruit woods, gentler than oak. Proper all-rounders.

HICKORY As American as apple pie and mispronouncing aluminium. Bold and unmistakable.

PECAN Nutty, mellow, slightly sweet. A softer hickory, that goes with everything.

TEXAS POST OAK The backbone of Texas BBQ. Oak with a peppery, vanilla edge.

MESQUITE Very strong. Use sparingly and only with beef.

MAPLE Sweet and subtle. Similar to cherry, great with pork and chicken.

TEMPERATURE VS TENDERNESS

Temperature is the guide, tenderness is the truth.

If your probe slides in like butter and the meat's wobbling like a waterbed in a 1980s motel but the thermometer's a few degrees off, you're done.

If it's hit the 'right' temperature but still feels tight, keep waiting.

For low-and-slow BBQ, fat, collagen, and connective tissue break down around 93–96°C/200–205°F. Meat won't pull or fall apart until it slowly reaches this range. That collagen turning into gelatine is where the magic happens, and it only happens with time and gentle heat.

RESTING - THE SECRET WEAPON

This is where restaurant-quality BBQ is made.

A brisket might take 12–15 hours to cook. Don't rush the rest. Holding meat above 63°C/145°F for several hours, or even overnight, turns good BBQ into something special.

Resting lets juices redistribute and the meat continue to tenderize. If your oven goes to 65°C/149°F, use it. If not, wrap the meat tightly, wrap it again in towels (or whatever you've got), stick it in a cool box and shut the lid. It'll hold heat for hours. Just make sure it stays above 63°C/145°F.

MULTI-CULTURAL BBQ

When approaching a book about Great British BBQ, it would be remiss not to dedicate a good chunk to the incredible impact and inspiration that people from all over the world have brought to British cookery, cuisine and culture. We are an island that has been defined by the people who have set foot here, lived here, worked here and contributed to the chaos and contradictions that make up our beautiful country.

Britain is internationally renowned and poked fun at as a country that invaded half the world for its spices then didn't bother to use any in its food. Nothing could be further from the truth. These days dishes like piri piri chicken, tikka masala or even the late-night kebab are as much a part of British culture and what it means to live in the UK as sticky toffee pudding or a Sunday roast.

For this section of the book we have reached out to some of the amazing businesses we know who are helping to bring incredible flavours from around the world to communities across the country. We have also spoken to members of our team at The Beefy Boys who have made Great Britain their home and who continue to help make The Beefy Boys what it is today, day in and day out. We could not do it without them.

We love Britain. We love the good bits, the bad bits, even the weather, and yes, even

Coldplay. We love the incredible cultural melting pot that can give you everything from Harry Potter to Trip Hop, from the *Antiques Roadshow* to Ozzy Osbourne, from Grime to The Beatles, from beans on toast to Balti curry.

A country that can be proud of its history but can also laugh at itself. A country that acknowledges the terrible things in its past while also recognizing the incredible amount of good achieved, not just at home but around the world as well. Great Britain is an amalgamation of all of us who inhabit it, all of us who live together, work together and, together, call it our home.

Long may Great Britain continue as the tolerant, innovative, chaotic and beautiful place it is today.

Serves: 6–8

BBQ setup: Rotisserie or 2-zone indirect grilling

Fuel source: Lumpwood, briquettes, or wood burnt down to embers

Cook time: 1 hour, plus overnight marinating

INGREDIENTS

For the chicken doner

430g (2 cups) Greek yoghurt

Juice of 2 lemons

2 tbsp salt

1 tbsp ground cumin

1½ tbsp smoked paprika

2 tbsp garlic granules

1 tbsp dried oregano

1 tsp ground black pepper

1½ tbsp Bovril

1 tbsp baking powder

20 boneless, skinless chicken thighs

For the fire pit chilli sauce

2 onions (unpeeled)

1 red (bell) pepper

2 assorted fresh chillies

400g (14oz) tomato pulp or chopped tomatoes

4 smoked garlic cloves (see page 154, or use regular)

1 tbsp fresh oregano leaves

1 tsp salt

1 tsp sugar

1 tbsp red wine vinegar

From Land's End to John o' Groats, the late-night kebab is a British institution. This Turkish import has become a tradition as intrinsic to our national identity as bonfire night, morris dancing, or forming queues. It's a known fact that a drunk Brit gravitates towards a kebab shop like a moth to a flame. It's instinct. We move as a herd from pub to club to kebab, floating towards the smells of vertically grilled meat like Thomas the cat floats to a freshly baked pie.

This recipe shows you how to recreate that culinary pilgrimage at home. And remember, when you're making or serving kebabs, you must refer to everyone as 'boss man'. That's just the rules (it's also been proven that this colloquial gesture of late-night friendship makes the food 50 percent more delicious).

Marinate the chicken. Combine all the chicken doner ingredients except the chicken in a large bowl. Add the chicken thighs and stir until fully coated. Cover and refrigerate overnight.

Build the kebab. The next day, get your rotisserie pole (if you have a rotisserie) and thread the thighs onto it, alternating the angle of each one so they criss-cross and stack neatly. Clamp tightly with the rotisserie forks. No rotisserie? No problem. You can use metal skewers to hold the chicken together, or even stack and cook it as a big kebab-log in a deep foil tray using the indirect side of your BBQ.

Cook the kebab. Set your BBQ up for rotisserie cooking, with hot coals on either side. If your BBQ has a lid, close it to help the chicken cook evenly. If not, it'll just take a little longer.

If using a rotisserie, keep the chicken spinning until it hits 75°C/167°F internal temperature, which should take about 45 minutes to 1 hour.

If you're not using a rotisserie, set up for 2-zone cooking. Place the chicken kebab in the cool zone and cook with the lid on until it reaches 70°C/158°F, then move it over the direct heat to caramelize the outer layers, turning every few minutes until it reaches 75°C/167°F internal temperature.

Recipe and ingredients continue...

For the smoked garlic sauce

4 smoked garlic cloves
(see page 154)
225g (1 cup) mayonnaise
225g (1 cup) sour cream
Juice of 1 lime
Pinch each of salt and ground
black pepper

For the grilled cabbage slaw

1 white cabbage
60ml (¼ cup) rapeseed (canola)
or olive (non-virgin) oil, plus
extra for grilling
1 tsp salt, plus extra for grilling
160ml (⅔ cup) cider vinegar
1 tsp sugar
1 tbsp chopped fresh mint
Bunch of parsley,
finely chopped
1 tsp dried oregano
½ tsp white pepper
4 pickled guindilla chillies,
finely chopped

For the pittas

240ml (1 cup) warm water
2 tsp fast-action dried yeast
½ tsp sugar
320g (2½ cups) plain
(all-purpose) flour, plus
extra for dusting
1 tsp salt

Make the fire pit chilli sauce. Place the onions, red pepper and chillies directly onto the coals. Turn them as each side blackens. Once roasted, peel away the charred skins, core the pepper and add all the flesh to a food processor along with the remaining ingredients. Blitz until smooth. Taste and adjust the seasoning or heat – if it needs more kick, add a few dashes of your favourite hot sauce.

Make the smoked garlic sauce. Add all the ingredients to a food processor and blitz until smooth. That's it. Smoky, creamy, delicious.

Prepare the grilled cabbage slaw. Cut the cabbage into wedges, lightly oil and season them, and grill over direct heat until the edges are beautifully charred. Remove and thinly slice. Toss the sliced cabbage with the measured oil, salt, cider vinegar, sugar, herbs, white pepper and chillies. The combo of smoky char, acidity and freshness cuts through the rich kebab meat perfectly.

Make the pittas. Combine the warm water, yeast, sugar, and 70g (½ cup) of the flour in a bowl. Whisk and leave for 30 minutes until it starts bubbling.

Add the remaining flour and the salt, and stir until a dough forms. Turn the dough out onto a lightly floured worktop and knead for a few minutes. Leave for 10 minutes, then knead again. Cover and leave in a warm place for 1 hour.

Divide the dough evenly into 8 pieces, roll each into a ball, and rest them for another 10 minutes. Roll each ball out flat on a flour-dusted work surface.

Cook the pittas in a hot cast-iron frying pan (skillet) or, if you are lucky enough to own one, a pizza oven. Once the bread starts to puff up, flip it and cook the other side. Don't worry if your pittas don't puff up perfectly – they'll still be delicious.

Assemble. Slice all your chicken off the skewer in thin strips and pile it onto a tray in the centre of the table. Warm your pittas, load them with chicken, slaw and your two sauces.

If you want to be *completely authentic*, attempt this recipe at 3am after an all-day drinking session, staggering around your garden while arguing about who's booking the Uber.

Serves: 2–4
BBQ setup: 2-zone direct grilling
Fuel source: Lumpwood, briquettes, or wood burnt down to embers
Cook time: 30 minutes, plus overnight marinating

INGREDIENTS

800g (1lb 12oz) flank steak or bavette
Rapeseed (canola) or peanut (groundnut) oil

For the suya rub

2 tbsp smooth peanut butter
80ml (⅓ cup) water
1 tbsp sweet paprika
1 tbsp rock salt (use half the volume if using table salt)
1 tbsp ground ginger
1 tbsp onion granules
1 tsp cayenne pepper
1 tsp garlic granules
½ tsp ground African cubeb pepper
¼ tsp ground cloves
1 tsp chicken powder

Beef suya is not a dish I was familiar with until I met Ezeke, our Senior Sous in Cheltenham. Ezeke hails originally from Nigeria; he came to the UK to study and started working with us on pot wash. His incredible work ethic and commitment to The Beefy Boys saw him shoot up the ladder to become the essential part of the team he is today. I am not exaggerating when I say he is one of the kindest, hardest-working and most genuine people I have ever met. Top bloke, and he has been kind enough to share his beef suya recipe with us.

Suya is the national dish of Nigeria and its peanut-based rub is absolutely delicious. You could use this rub on fries, chicken or fish, not just the beef in this recipe. Ezeke sent me so much information about what suya means to him, its origins and how much it reminds him of home. I wish I had space to include it all. That is the amazing thing about food – its ability to inspire us, to connect us to our history and ancestors, but also to act as a bridge to new friends and new places. Thanks for the recipe, Ezeke.

Preheat the oven to 120°C/250°F/Gas ½. Mix the peanut butter with the water until smooth. Pour the mixture onto a baking tray and bake it for 20–30 minutes or until the mixture has completely dried out. Once dry, blitz in a food processor to a fine powder.

Mix the peanut butter powder with the remaining rub ingredients.

Slice your steak against the grain into long strips. Add a splash of oil and season generously with your suya rub. Mix well so every strip is coated and leave to marinate in the fridge overnight.

Get your BBQ ready for direct grilling and oil up the grates well. Fold each strip of beef onto a skewer, like a concertina, so it has lots of surface area for caramelization.

Sear the kebabs all over, turning regularly. Once they reach an internal temperature of 52–55°C/125–131°F, it is time to take them off.

Allow the kebabs to rest for a few minutes before serving.

INGREDIENTS

500g (1lb 2oz) boneless, skinless chicken breast or thighs, cut into 2.5cm (1 inch) strips

For the marinade

½ tbsp fish sauce

1 tbsp oyster sauce

1 tbsp sugar

3 tbsp ground turmeric

1 tbsp light soy sauce

For the peanut dipping sauce

50ml (3½ tbsp) vegetable oil

100g (3½oz) massaman curry paste

50g (1¾oz) peanuts

100ml (generous ⅓ cup) coconut milk

70g (2½oz) sugar

For the Thai cucumber salad

1 banana shallot, thinly sliced into rings

Juice of 2 limes

1 large cucumber, thinly sliced

2 garlic cloves, crushed with a pinch of rock salt

20g (¾oz) coriander (cilantro), finely chopped

20g (¾oz) Thai basil, finely chopped

3 tbsp fish sauce

2 tsp sugar

2 tsp salt

½ tsp MSG

1 tsp chilli crisp

Everyone loves Thai food… apart from those people born with that weird coriander (cilantro) reaction thing (there's no coriander in the chicken here, just the salad, so you're all good, my abnormal tastebud friends). We are lucky enough to have an amazing Thai takeaway in Hereford called Thaitastic Thai, run by incredible Thai chef Aree and her husband (chief washer-up) Steve. They serve freshly cooked, properly prepared Thai food, and many a Beefy Boys lunch break has been saved by their incredible dishes.

Thai food is huge in the UK. As a nation we love curry, and Thai food – with its fragrant pastes and fresh sauces – has become a national favourite. We had to reach out to Aree and Steve to get a BBQ-friendly Thai recipe into the book, and you just can't beat a bit of Thai chicken satay. Check out Aree's recipe below, alongside our Beefy Boys Thai-style cucumber salad.

In a large bowl, mix all the marinade ingredients together, then add the chicken strips, coating well. Cover and refrigerate overnight.

For the dipping sauce, heat the oil and massaman paste in a pan over a low heat. Combine the peanuts and coconut milk in a blender or food processor, and blend until smooth. Pour this into the massaman paste, add the sugar and stir well. Simmer over a medium heat until thickened, then set aside to cool.

For the cucumber salad, place the sliced shallot in a small bowl and squeeze over the lime juice to lightly pickle. Add the cucumber to a mixing bowl with the pickled shallots, then add the crushed garlic along with the herbs, fish sauce, sugar, salt and MSG. Toss everything together and finish with the chilli crisp.

Thread the chicken onto your skewers (if using bamboo skewers, soak them in water for a few hours first).

Set your BBQ for 2-zone cooking and get it nice and hot (the 2-second hand rule, see page 32). BBQ or grill the chicken skewers for 2–3 minutes each side until cooked through and lightly charred.

Serve with the peanut sauce for dipping, with the cucumber salad alongside.

Serves: 4

BBQ setup: 2-zone direct grilling

Fuel source: Lumpwood, briquettes, or wood burnt down to embers

Cook time: 30 minutes, plus optional overnight marinating and 1½ hours for the naan

INGREDIENTS

800g (1lb 12oz) chicken thigh fillets, cut lengthways into 5cm (2 inch) strips

Melted butter, to finish (optional)

For the marinade

1 tbsp ginger paste

1 tsp garlic paste

¼ tsp ground fennel

Juice of 1 lemon

80g (⅓ cup) Greek yoghurt

1 tbsp grated mozzarella

1 tbsp double (heavy) cream

½ tsp ground cardamom

½ tsp ground coriander

½ tsp ground black pepper

1 tsp garam masala

½ tsp ground cumin

1 tsp chaat masala

¼ tsp ground nutmeg

¼ tsp fenugreek powder

Handful of chopped coriander (cilantro) leaves

¼ tsp salt

1 tbsp dry-roasted gram flour

1 tbsp neutral oil

For the tikka sauce

3–4 tbsp rapeseed (canola) oil

A little butter

1 large white onion, halved and sliced into half-moons

3 tbsp Greek yoghurt

I don't think it should ever be overlooked what a cultural landmark chicken tikka masala is. Chicken tikka masala is a dish that sounds truly Indian but was, in fact, invented in an Indian curry house in Glasgow in the 1970s. What a shiny example of cultures integrating and innovating, and what an incredible dish chicken tikka masala is, with its grilled meats and rich, deep sauce. To make sure we had a recipe to do this iconic piece of history justice, we reached out to an amazing local chef we know: Suki Pantal, founder of Suki's Curries and Spices.

Suki is based in Worcestershire and originally hails from New Delhi. Her knowledge of regional Indian cookery is second to none. She's sorted us out with this amazing chicken tikka and naan recipe – and these naan (see overleaf) are the best I've ever tasted.

Mix all the marinade ingredients together in a bowl. Add the chicken, coat well and refrigerate for at least 1 hour, ideally overnight.

Thread each strip of chicken onto a skewer by looping it back on itself as if you are sewing. This stops the meat spinning when it hits the grill.

Set your BBQ up for 2-zone hot and fast direct grilling, using the 2-second hand rule (see page 32). Grill the skewers over a high heat to colour and char, turning as needed, and moving to the cooler zone if necessary so they cook through and stay juicy. Take them off the grill once they hit 75°C/167°F internal temperature. Brush with melted butter right at the end, if you like, for that proper tikka finish.

For the sauce, heat a tablespoon of oil and a little butter in a pan, add the onion and cook over a medium heat for 20–30 minutes until caramelized. Leave to cool a little, then add to a blender with the yoghurt and fresh coriander and blitz to a smooth paste.

Recipe and ingredients continue...

Handful of coriander (cilantro) leaves

2–3 green cardamom pods

1 black cardamom pod

1–2 cloves

2.5cm (1 inch) piece of cinnamon stick

1 tsp ginger and garlic paste

1 tsp Kashmiri chilli powder

1 tsp chaat masala

½ tsp ground black pepper

½ tsp ground turmeric

60ml (¼ cup) milk

240ml (1 cup) warm water

To garnish

½ tsp garam masala

1 tsp dried fenugreek leaves, crushed

Heat 2–3 tablespoons of oil and a teaspoon of butter in a non-stick pan. Add the whole spices and let them crackle and release their fragrance, then add the ginger and garlic paste and cook until the raw smell disappears. Stir in the onion and yoghurt paste and cook for a few minutes.

Reduce the heat and add the chilli powder, chaat masala, black pepper and turmeric. Pour in the milk and warm water, increase the heat back to medium and cook until the sauce thickens and the oil begins to separate.

Add your cooked chicken and turn gently in the sauce until everything is coated. Adjust the seasoning, adding salt to taste.

Finish with the garam masala and crushed fenugreek leaves.

Note If you don't want whole spices in the sauce, scoop them out before adding the pastes. Or grind them and add them later with the powdered spices.

Makes: 4

INGREDIENTS

250g (1¾ cups plus 2 tbsp) strong white bread flour

½ tsp salt

150ml (scant ⅔ cup) warm water

1 tsp sugar

1 tsp fast-action dried yeast

1 tsp neutral oil or butter, plus extra for drizzling and frying

1 tbsp chopped coriander (cilantro) leaves

½ tsp onion seeds (kalonji)

Garlic butter, to finish (optional)

NAAN BREADS

These cook up great in a roaring-hot wood-fired oven, or set your BBQ up for BBQ roasting and use a pizza stone. You can also set your BBQ up for direct grilling and grill the naans over the heat or, if you are feeling super-brave, blow the ash off some red-hot lumpwood and throw directly on the coals.

Mix the flour and salt in a bowl. Combine the warm water with the sugar and yeast and stir to dissolve. Add this to the flour along with the teaspoon of oil or butter. Mix into a loose, sticky dough. Add a little more flour if needed, then knead until smooth, cover and rest for 30 minutes.

Divide the dough into 4 portions and shape each into a tight ball. Roll the first ball into an oval shape. Sprinkle over some coriander and onion seeds, then add a drizzle of oil on top and press lightly so it all sticks.

Heat a non-stick frying pan, skillet or tawa over a medium heat and add 2 tablespoons of oil. Place the naan in the pan, topping-side up and cook until bubbles form. Flip, cook for 30–40 seconds, flip back to the other side and press the edges with a spatula for even cooking.

Remove and brush with garlic butter, if you fancy. Repeat with the rest of the dough and serve hot.

Serves: 2–4

BBQ setup: 2-zone direct grilling or smoking

Fuel source: Lumpwood, briquettes, or wood burnt down to embers

Wood flavour: Pimento wood if you can get it, cherry if you can't

Cook time: 1 hour, plus overnight marinating

INGREDIENTS

1 whole chicken, quartered

For the jerk marinade

3 spring onions (scallions), roughly chopped

8 garlic cloves, peeled

1 thumb-sized piece of fresh ginger, peeled (bear in mind I have unusually big thumbs from years of Mario Kart abuse), roughly chopped

2 tbsp thyme leaves

2 tbsp ground allspice

1 tsp ground cinnamon

1 red onion, quartered

At least 2 Scotch bonnet chillies (but add as many as you want)

2 tbsp smoked salt

1 tbsp brown sugar

2 tbsp Worcestershire sauce

1 tbsp cracked black pepper

380ml (1½ cups) soy sauce

240ml (1 cup) orange juice

Juice of 2 limes

60ml (¼ cup) olive (non-virgin) or rapeseed (canola) oil

We love Caribbean food. It was never readily available in our home town of Hereford but whenever we were in cities like Bristol or London, we always used to make a beeline for anywhere serving proper jerk chicken, curry goat or salt fish and ackee. We were over the moon when the street food pop-up Jerk Bay started in Hereford. Lamin and the team at Jerk Bay are total legends, banging out incredibly tasty and authentic Jamaican street food, so we had to get some tips off them for our Jerk recipe.

Blitz all the marinade ingredients in a food processor.

Grab a ziplock bag, place the chicken pieces inside and pour in three-quarters of the marinade. Keep the remaining separate from the raw meat and save it for later as a dipping sauce.

Rub the marinade all over the chicken. Lift the skin where you can and massage the marinade between the skin and the meat. Leave to marinate in the fridge for a minimum of 24 hours.

To cook the chicken you can either cook it indirect, away from the direct heat, turning regularly and letting the gentle heat of the coals slowly cook the chicken, or you can smoke it over pimento or cherry wood. If smoking, get your smoker running between 120 and 150°C/250 and 300°F.

Whichever method you use, remove the breast when it has been reading above 65°C/149°F for 10 minutes; bear in mind that carryover cooking should take a piece of chicken removed at 65°C potentially all the way up to the late 60s°C/150°F once removed off the grill. The thigh and leg can be taken all the way to the high 80s/192°F or early 90s/195°F and will still be juicy.

Serve with the reserved marinade as a dipping sauce.

Lamin's TOP TIPS for Jerk Chicken

- Marinate the chicken at least overnight to allow the flavours to fully penetrate.
- Scoring the chicken helps the seasoning get into every bit of the meat.
- Cook the chicken over indirect heat or in a smoker to get that smoky flavour and tender texture.
- Scotch bonnets are key in the making of jerk seasoning. The more you add, the spicier it gets. Note that they are incredibly hot, so be careful with the quantity you use.

Serves: 2–4

BBQ setup: 2-zone direct grilling

Fuel source: Lumpwood, briquettes, or wood burnt down to embers

Cook time: 30 minutes, plus optional overnight marinating and 1–2 days for the marinade to mature

INGREDIENTS

15–20 chicken wings

For the whisky piri piri marinade

250ml (1 cup) olive oil

8 dried bird's eye chillies

6 garlic cloves, peeled

7 bay leaves

1½ tbsp black peppercorns

2 large fresh red chillies

3 tbsp whisky

Juice of 1 lemon

2 tbsp red wine vinegar

2 tbsp smoked rock salt

Piri piri has become an institution in the UK. It blew up in the 2010s when Nando's took over the high streets and spawned countless other piri piri shops.

For this recipe we reached out to a legend of our Hereford restaurant, the one and only Joe Pinho. Joe originally hails from Portugal and he is one of the bedrocks of our Hereford team: incredibly caring, passionate, funny and with a commitment to service and our customers that is unmatched. Joe's family recipe is so moreish and delicious that once you make it you will not make it any other way again.

For the marinade, pour the olive oil into a pan and add the chillies, garlic, bay leaves, peppercorns and whole fresh chillies. Set the pan over a low heat. You will start to smell incredible aromas and you will hear the bay leaves and chillies begin to pop and crackle.

Let the mixture gently infuse for 10–15 minutes. Keep an eye on it; you don't want the garlic to burn, just lightly colour.

Once you are happy with the colour, add the whisky, lemon juice, vinegar and smoked salt. Stir everything together and remove from the heat. Allow the mixture to cool to room temperature, then pour into a food processor and blitz. Transfer to a jar and rest it in the fridge, ideally for 1 or 2 days to mature.

Prepare your wings however you like them – whole or separated into drums and flats. Mix them with two-thirds of the marinade and leave them to marinate overnight in the fridge.

The next day, fire up your BBQ for 2-zone direct grilling. You want a medium heat, about a 3–4 second hand rule (see page 32). Place the wings on the grill and let them sit for 2–3 minutes before turning. As you turn them, brush with more of the leftover marinade, keeping some aside to serve as a dipping sauce. Keep turning and brushing every couple of minutes until you have beautiful colour on the wings and they read at least 75°C/167°F. Because they are wings, you can take them all the way into the 90s/190s and they will still be juicy.

Serve the wings hot with the reserved marinade as a dipping sauce.

Serves: 2–4

BBQ setup: 2-zone direct grilling

Fuel source: Lumpwood, briquettes, or wood burnt down to embers

Cook time: 30 minutes, plus overnight soaking then overnight marinating

INGREDIENTS

1kg (2lb 4oz) flanken-cut beef ribs, 1cm (½ inch) thick

For the bulgogi marinade

350g (12oz) ripe pears, cored and peeled

220g (7¾oz) white onions, diced (prepped weight)

150g (5½oz) fresh ginger, roughly chopped

50g (1¾oz) peeled garlic

300ml (1¼ cups) light soy sauce

150ml (scant ⅔ cup) mirin

20g (¾oz) sugar

½ tsp ground black pepper

20ml (1½ tbsp) oil

For the dipping sauce

1 tbsp sesame oil

A good pinch of rock salt

Pinch of cracked black pepper

The first time I tried Korean BBQ I was blown away. It completely opened my eyes to what BBQ can be. We're lucky enough to have an awesome independent Korean BBQ restaurant in our UK hometown, run by Pampi and Peyman. They also have an incredible steak restaurant called En Steak in Hereford and another site in Birmingham. They make absolutely faultless food, so we had to get their help with a classic LA galbi, or UK galbi – flanken-cut beef short ribs tenderized in a pear and soy marinade.

Ask your butcher to cut your flanken ribs about 1cm (½ inch) thick, or order them online if needed.

Before marinating, soak the ribs in cold water overnight. This helps draw out any impurities that can affect the flavour of the final marinade. (If you're using this marinade on other cuts of beef, you can skip this step.)

For the marinade, add all the ingredients to a food processor and blitz until smooth. Pour the marinade over the ribs, making sure everything is well coated. Refrigerate overnight.

The next day, remove the ribs from the marinade and shake off any excess. For the dipping sauce, spoon the sesame oil into a small dish and add the salt and black pepper.

Set your BBQ up for 2-zone hot and fast direct grilling; you want to get a really good char on these with nice little gnarly, crispy bits. Grill the ribs over a medium heat, turning often. These will be delicious anywhere from medium rare (around 55°C/131°F internal temperature) to well done – the marbling keeps them juicy either way.

Serve with sliced chillies, spring onions and sesame seeds as a garnish, if you fancy. Dip your grilled flanken-cut ribs into the dipping sauce and get stuck in!

Serves: 2–4

BBQ setup: 2-zone direct grilling (optional BBQ roasting)

Fuel source: Lumpwood, briquettes, or wood burnt down to embers

Cook time: 2 hours if making your own tortillas, 30 minutes if not, plus overnight marinating

INGREDIENTS

1.2kg (2lb 10oz) flank steak

For the carne asada marinade

180ml (¾ cup) orange juice

120ml (½ cup) lemon juice

80ml (⅓ cup) lime juice

4 garlic cloves, minced

120ml (½ cup) light soy sauce

1 tsp finely chopped chipotle pepper from a can

1 tbsp chilli powder

1 tbsp ground cumin

1 tbsp paprika

1 tsp dried oregano

1 tbsp black pepper

Bunch of coriander (cilantro), chopped

120ml (½ cup) olive oil

Tacos are great. Delicious meat and sauces wrapped in little flour or corn tortillas – the perfect street-food delivery system. Our sous chef Nathan in Shrewsbury originally hails from Mexico and he has been kind enough to work with us on this recipe. Nathan is a true legend and brings his heart and soul and incredible sense of humour to the restaurant. He is also a great chef who loves a touch of spice, even if he does need reminding now and then that British tastebuds are not quite as robust as the good people of Mexico's against chilli.

Marinate the steak. Place all the marinade ingredients in a blender and blitz until smooth. Pour over the flank steak, massage it in, and chill overnight.

Make the salsa roja. Add all the salsa ingredients to a blender and blitz until smooth. Tip into a saucepan and simmer over a low heat for 10 minutes.

Make the beef fat tortillas. Heat the butter, beef dripping and water in a pan until melted. Add the flour, baking powder and smoked salt to a mixing bowl, then pour the hot liquid over the flour and knead into a smooth dough. Set aside and let it rest for 1 hour.

Portion the dough into 8–12 balls, depending on how big you want your tacos. Flatten each one and cook individually in a pan with a little beef dripping until lightly golden.

Cook the steak. Set your BBQ up for 2-zone direct grilling. Sear the steak hard over the hot side, then finish on the cooler side. Pull it at 52–55°C/125–131°F, rest for a minute, then slice thinly across the grain.

Build the tacos. Spread salsa roja on a tortilla. Add slices of steak. Crumble over the queso fresco or feta and top with white onion, coriander and a squeeze of lime.

For the salsa roja

5 ripe beef tomatoes, roughly chopped

3 smoked garlic cloves (see page 154), peeled

Pinch of salt

3 jalapeño chillies, roughly chopped

½ onion, roughly chopped

2 tbsp olive (non-virgin) or rapeseed (canola) oil

Juice of 2 limes

Large handful of coriander (cilantro), roughly chopped

For the beef fat tortillas

1 tbsp unsalted butter

1 tbsp beef dripping, plus extra for frying

180ml (¾ cup) water

260g (2 cups) plain (all-purpose) flour

2 tsp baking powder

1 tsp smoked salt

For the garnishes

Queso fresco or feta

Finely chopped white onion

Finely chopped coriander (cilantro)

Lime wedges

Serves: 2–4

BBQ setup: 2-zone direct grilling

Fuel source: Lumpwood, briquettes, or wood burnt down to embers

Cook time: 30 minutes, plus overnight marinating

1kg (2lb 4oz) pork neck fillet

1 medium onion

120ml (½ cup) kefir

2 tbsp sunflower or olive oil

2½ tsp salt

1 tsp ground black pepper

For the adjika

500g (1lb 2oz) tomatoes, roughly chopped

250g (9oz) sweet (bell) peppers, roughly chopped

1–2 hot red chillies, to taste, roughly chopped

3 garlic cloves, peeled

½ tbsp salt

½ tbsp sugar

1 tbsp red wine vinegar

2 tbsp sunflower or olive oil

One of the things we love about BBQ, apart from the flavours, the fire and being outdoors, is how it brings people together. That is true of every food culture on earth.

Dmytro is one of our chefs in Hereford and is originally from Ukraine. He is one of the most reliable, hard-working members of our team, always at work with a smile on his face, banging out great food day after day. A true legend in The Beefy Boys' kitchens.

BBQ brings back fond memories of home for Dmytro. Just like in the UK, BBQs are huge gatherings in Ukraine, where friends and family gather around fire and food to share stories, laugh and enjoy each other's company away from the chaos of the world.

For Dmytro, BBQ back home means shashlyk – marinated skewers of meat cooked over hot coals. For this recipe we have gone with pork and we are serving it with adjika, a traditional fiery Ukrainian pepper and tomato sauce.

Cut the pork into pieces about 4cm (1½ inches) thick – you don't want the pieces too small or they will dry out. Slice the onion into rings and lightly squeeze with your hands to release the juices.

In a large bowl, mix the pork with the onion, kefir, oil, salt and pepper. Massage everything together with your hands, gently pressing the onions to release more juice into the meat. Cover and refrigerate for at least 6 hours, ideally overnight.

For the adjika, put the tomatoes, peppers, chillies and garlic into in a food processor and blitz to a thick paste. Add the salt, sugar, vinegar and oil and mix well. Place in the fridge overnight to allow the flavours to develop.

Set your BBQ up for 2-zone direct grilling over a medium heat. You want a 3–4 second hand rule (see page 32).

Skewer the meat, threading the pieces tightly together so they stay juicy. Grill for 15–20 minutes, turning regularly until golden brown with a bit of char and reading around 70–75°C/158–167°F internal temperature.

Serve with the adjika on the side.

SAUCES

SMOKED APPLE BUTTER

INGREDIENTS

1.2kg (2lb 10oz) cooking apples
1 star anise
1 cinnamon stick
50g (3½ tbsp) butter

Set your BBQ up for smoking at 120°C/250°F.
Core the apples (leave the skin on if you like) and
smoke them for 20–25 minutes until softened and
lightly golden. Allow them to cool slightly, then
roughly chop and place in a pan with the star
anise, cinnamon stick, and half the butter. Heat
gently for about 10 minutes, then pour everything
into a food processor, add the remaining butter
and blitz to a smooth purée. Taste it: depending
on your apples, you might want to add a bit of
sugar for sweetness or cider vinegar for balance.

SMOKED ORANGE KETCHUP

INGREDIENTS

2 oranges
1 tbsp sugar
1 tbsp golden syrup
¾ tsp salt

Peel the oranges and smoke at 120°C/250°F for
30 minutes over oak, apple or cherry. Blitz the
oranges with the sugar, golden syrup and salt,
transfer to a saucepan and bring to the boil.
Bubble it for 5–10 minutes, skimming off any
froth that rises, until thickened, then remove
from the heat and chill.

CHAR TARTARE

INGREDIENTS

1 shallot, peeled
2 lemons
2 tbsp dill, chopped
1 tbsp finely chopped parsley
225g (1 cup) mayonnaise
1 tsp Dijon mustard
40g (1½oz) capers
55g (2oz) gherkins, finely diced
2 smoked garlic cloves (see page 154),
crushed to a paste with a little salt

Slice the shallot and lemons in half and grill them
over a high heat until charred. When cool enough
to handle, finely dice the shallot.

Mix the herbs with the mayo, mustard, capers and
gherkins, then stir in the garlic paste.

Mix in the diced shallot. Taste and adjust salt and
acidity with a squeeze of charred lemon. This sauce
gets even better after sitting in the fridge overnight.

HEREFORDIAN WHITE SAUCE

INGREDIENTS

225g (1 cup) mayonnaise
110g (½ cup) salad cream
1 tsp garlic granules
2 tsp salt
1 tbsp honey
120ml (½ cup) cider vinegar
½ tsp dried sage
½ tsp dried thyme
½ tsp ground black pepper

Mix all your ingredients for the
sauce in a bowl, and serve.

RED PEPPER DIP

INGREDIENTS

350g (12oz) roasted red peppers in oil (from a can or jar), or homemade (see method below)
1 garlic clove, peeled
Juice of 1 lemon
1 fresh chilli (optional)
Olive oil (if using homemade roasted peppers)
Salt and ground black pepper

If roasting the peppers yourself, char them on the grill, then throw into a bowl and cover with cling film (plastic wrap), let them steam, then peel off the outer skin. A little charred skin left on is okay. Remove the seeds and tops, then blitz in a food processor with the garlic, lemon juice, chilli (if using), oil and seasoning until smooth.

If using canned or jarred peppers, add them and their oil to a food processor with the garlic, lemon juice, chilli (if using) and seasoning. If you like a bit of heat, any variety of chilli will work and each will add its own flavour and unique taste to the dip.

HOT HONEY

INGREDIENTS

240ml (1 cup) runny honey
½ tbsp cayenne pepper
½ tbsp chilli powder
2 tbsp buffalo sauce (or your favourite hot sauce)
1 tbsp sriracha

Add all the ingredients to a pan and stir over a medium heat until combined and the spices have dissolved into the honey.

BLUE MONDAY SAUCE

INGREDIENTS

2 tbsp butter
2 tbsp plain (all-purpose) flour
280ml (2 cups) milk
80ml (⅓ cup) white wine
180g (6¼oz) Blue Monday cheese
1 tsp each of salt and ground black pepper
½ tsp English mustard
60ml (¼ cup) cider vinegar

In a saucepan, melt the butter and flour together to form a roux. Stir constantly for about 5 minutes to cook out the flour, then gradually whisk in the milk, a little at a time, until you've got a smooth, lump-free béchamel.

Pour in the wine and keep it bubbling gently for another 5 minutes to cook off the alcohol. Crumble in the blue cheese and stir until melted through. Add the salt, pepper, mustard and cider vinegar, then taste and adjust the seasoning to your liking.

BREAD SAUCE

INGREDIENTS

500ml (2 cups) milk
1 medium onion, peeled
10 black peppercorns
1 cinnamon stick
1 star anise
2 bay leaves (fresh or dried)
225g (8oz) white bread, blitzed into crumbs
2 tbsp salted butter
½ tsp salt
5 tbsp double (heavy) cream

Add the milk, onion, peppercorns, cinnamon, star anise and bay leaves to a pan. Bring to a gentle simmer for 10 minutes. Remove the aromatics, then add the breadcrumbs, butter, salt and cream. Stir until thickened; keep warm.

DIRTY DIANE SAUCE

INGREDIENTS

1 banana shallot
3 smoked garlic cloves (see page 154)
or regular garlic
100g (3½oz) chestnut mushrooms
1 tbsp beef fat (the garlic-and rosemary-infused
beef fat from page 155 would be perfect) or butter
1 generous shot of brandy
1 tsp Dijon mustard
1 tsp Bovril
1 tbsp Worcestershire sauce
150ml (scant ⅔ cup) double (heavy) cream
Pinch of salt and a few good twists of black pepper

Finely dice the shallot and smoked garlic. Slice the mushrooms thinly.

Heat the beef fat (or butter) in a pan. Fry the mushrooms for 3–4 minutes, then add the shallot and garlic, cooking for another 5 minutes until softened and smelling amazing.

Take the pan off the heat. Add the brandy, return to the heat, and carefully light it to flambé and burn off the alcohol. Try not to set your eyebrows on fire. (Top tip: redraw your eyebrows on with a piece of coal from the BBQ, making sure it has cooled down first.)

Stir in the mustard, Bovril, Worcestershire sauce and cream. Let it bubble nicely before seasoning with salt and pepper.

GOLDEN CHIPOTLE SYRUP

INGREDIENTS

240ml (1 cup) golden syrup
1 tbsp dried chipotle chilli flakes

Add the syrup and chipotle flakes to a small pan over a medium heat and simmer gently for 15 minutes.

CHAMP MAYO

INGREDIENTS

2 tbsp finely diced spring onion (scallion)
3 tbsp mayonnaise

Mix the spring onion and mayonnaise together in a small bowl and set aside.

WHISKY MAYO

INGREDIENTS

2 tbsp mayonnaise
1 tbsp green peppercorns
1 smoked garlic clove (see page 154),
crushed to a purée with rock salt
1 tsp Dijon mustard
A good dash of whisky, to taste

Combine all the ingredients in a small bowl or jar. Stir well and adjust the whisky to taste (go carefully unless you want a burger that fails a breathalyzer).

LEMON PEPPER MAYO

INGREDIENTS

1 lemon
225g (1 cup) mayonnaise
½ tbsp freshly cracked black pepper
Pinch of salt

Slice the lemon in half and char it directly over the heat. Let it cool, then squeeze the juice into the mayonnaise. Stir through the cracked black pepper and salt.

GLAZES

GUINNESS GLAZE

INGREDIENTS

240ml (1 cup) Guinness
1 tbsp tomato purée (paste)
1 tbsp light brown sugar
2 tbsp Worcestershire sauce
80g (⅓ cup) tomato ketchup
1 tbsp American mustard
3 tbsp light soy sauce
½ tsp salt
1 tsp garlic granules
½ tsp ground white pepper

Add the Guinness to a saucepan over a high heat and reduce by one-third. Then stir in the rest of the ingredients and cook until smooth and glossy.

BBQ SAUCE GLAZE

INGREDIENTS

240ml (1 cup) brown ale (we use Butty Bach)
240ml (1 cup) tomato ketchup
60ml (¼ cup) brown sauce
60ml (¼ cup) puréed chipotles
60ml (¼ cup) American mustard
2 tbsp Worcestershire sauce
120ml (½ cup) honey
2 tbsp light soy sauce
1 tbsp smoked paprika

Add the ale to a pan and reduce by half, then add all the remaining ingredients and stir until smooth. Simmer for a few minutes and it is ready to use

WORCESTERSHIRE SAUCE GLAZE

INGREDIENTS

120ml (½ cup) Worcestershire sauce
80ml (⅓ cup) golden syrup
65g (⅓ cup) light brown sugar

Add the ingredients to a pan over a medium heat and bubble away until the Worcestershire has reduced and the sauce has started to become sticky.

MARMALADE BBQ GLAZE

INGREDIENTS

340g (1 cup) marmalade
170g (½ cup) honey
80ml (⅓ cup) orange juice
80g (⅓ cup) tomato ketchup
2 tsp salt
½ tsp cayenne pepper
2 tbsp apple cider vinegar

Add all the ingredients to a saucepan and stir over a medium heat until combined. Let it bubble for a couple of minutes, stirring, then set aside.

porkerhouse chop with rhubarb and
     mustard ketchup 122
  saddle of pork with smoked apple
     butter 54
  smoked pork belly 168
  Ukrainian shashlyk with adjika 212
potatoes: bicarb brined spit chicken
     46
  bone marrow mash cottage pie 50
  breakfast potatoes 36
  chips 58
  hot pot potatoes 42
prawn (jumbo shrimp) cocktail,
     grilled 56–7

Q

quail: the game tray 80–2

R

ranch slaw, salad cream 158
resting 189
reverse sear 100–1
rhubarb and mustard ketchup 122
roasting: BBQ roasting 24–5
  spit roasting 25, 30
rotisserie 25, 30

S

sage and garlic basting butter 80–2
salad cream: Herefordian white sauce
     214
  salad cream ranch dressing 158
salads: grilled cabbage slaw 192–4
  salad cream ranch slaw 158
  Thai cucumber salad 198
salsa roja 210–11
salsa verde 66–9
salt 90
  SPG 33
Santa Maria grills 18
sauces 214–16
sausages: butter-basted stuffed spit
     chicken 72–3
  craft sausage making 90–3
  full English BBQ breakfast 36
  the game tray 80–2

searing: forward sear 100–1
  reverse sear 100–1, 102
  sear-pause-repeat 100–1, 102
seasoning 104, 188
shashlik: Ukrainian shashlyk with
     adjika 212
Shrewsbury sauce 86
skewers: BBQ beef suya Nigerian beef
     skewers 196
  Thai chicken skewers 198
  Ukrainian shashlyk 212
slaws: grilled cabbage slaw 192–4
  salad cream ranch slaw 158
smoke: good smoke vs dirty smoke
     26, 188
smoked apple butter 214
smoked beetroot 152
  smoked beetroot ketchup 153
smoked Brit churri 108
smoked confit oxtail 180
smoked garlic 154
  smoked garlic sauce 192–4
smoked mint churri 126
smoked orange ketchup 214
smoked patties 142
smoked pork belly 168
smokers 18, 25
Sosij 90–3
spatulas 23
SPG 33, 93
spit cooking 25, 30
steak 94–119
  anatomy of a great steak 98
  how to cook 100–2
  picking your steak 94
  prepping your steak 94–7
  see also beef for individual types
     of steak
stick burners 18
surf and turf with Beefy Boy butter
     114
suya rub 196
swede (rutabaga): pickled neeps 136
syrup, golden chipotle 216

T

tacos, carne asada 210–11
temperature: hand rule 32
  temperature vs tenderness 189
temperature probes 23
Thai chicken skewers 198
Thai cucumber salad 198
Thor's hammer with mac and cheese
     176
tomatoes: adjika 212
  fire pit chilli sauce 192–4
  full English BBQ breakfast 36
  salsa roja 210–11
tongs 23
tools 22–3
tortillas, beef fat 210–11
Tunley, Ashley 164–7
turkey breast, maple brined 182

U

UK galbi Korean beef short ribs 208
Ukrainian shashlyk with adjika 212

V

vegetables: grilled vegetables 66–9
  veg platter 148
venison: cocoa venison kebab 60
  the game tray 80–2

W

Wagyu brisket Texas style 187
Welsh rarebit burger cheese 138
wet brining 27
whisky: whisky mayo 216
  whisky piri piri marinade 206
wild boar: the game tray 80–2
wild garlic butter picanha 120
wood 20
  for smoke 189
wood chip boxes 23
wood-fired ovens 18
Worcestershire sauce: Welsh rarebit
     burger cheese 138
  Worcestershire sauce glaze 217

Well, if you've got this far, you've either read this book from cover to cover, or you've jumped straight to the back looking for an email address to request a refund. Either way, thank you for taking the time to pick this book up and read it. We genuinely hope it's inspired you in some way to get outdoors, light a fire, and get cooking.

We are incredibly lucky to be able to take our hobby and passion and turn it into a living. None of the mad ideas, questionable decisions, long cooks, late nights, or general Beefy Boys chaos would be possible without the support of a huge number of people around us.

A huge thank you to some of the people who helped make this book happen. Jim, for building the outdoor kitchen we cooked it all in. Murf's brother Steve, for sourcing us some incredible game alongside Brendan Sprocket. John from Birchwood Firewood & Charcoal, for top-notch charcoal and wood. Jon Finch and the whole Weber team, Kristo at Kadai, and the entire team at Firepits UK.

Massive thanks to Neil Powell Master Butchers and the legend that is Andy 'Joner' Jones. A huge shout-out to all the boys and girls at Heggies of Hereford, who went above and beyond supporting this book with some incredible steaks, chops, and roasting joints. Big thanks to Warrendale Wagyu for the unbelievable tomahawks and picanhas. Thank you as well to Hanks' Meat & Game in Ross-on-Wye, for the incredible boar and venison sausages. Peter Cook, thank you for the great buns!

Thank you to Alan Quartermain for the awesome illustrations, Pete for the incredible photography, and our super-patient editor Stacey, who is the real hero here. And, of course, Murf's beautiful wife Jo, who pulled the whole design together.

Huge thanks to the Beefy Boys' resident pitmaster Ashley from Big Smoke BBQ, who contributed across all the smoking recipes in this book. Massive thanks to everyone who shared recipes and knowledge with us: Alasdair from Sosij, Suki, Joe Pinho, Nath, Ezeke, Aree, Pampi, Lamin, and Dmytro. Big thanks as well to the Beefstock and Nozstock teams for all the support. Huge thank you to Alec From Meat City Smokers for the incredible direct heat Hog reactor. A massive thanks also to some of the guys who helped out but we didn't have space for their recipes in the end – thank you, Yen and Arnold, it was delicious, but we ran out of room!

We have to give an enormous thank you to our entire team at The Beefy Boys. You are all incredible. This simply does not work without you, and it is a genuine joy to work alongside every single one of you.

We'd also like to thank our families: Jo, Kate, Nicola, Archie, Poppy, Bill, Ted, Edie, Frank, Matilda, Parker, Bezza, Di, Lyndsay, Jill, John ME, John S, Steve, Jason, Aaron, Pete, Caroline, Lilly and Mia.

Finally, thank you to the people whose advice we've sought while writing this book and who have supported us through all the mad things we do: DJ BBQ, Tom Kerridge, Sam and Shauna, Martin Dobbs, Simon Blagden, Paul Alexander, David Sykes, Henry Wilson, Marcus Bawden, and Robert Gwynn Palmer.

And last of all, thank you to the good people of Hereford, and to every single person who has ever bought a burger: you are the reason we are here and we will forever be in your debt.

BEEF
STOCK
BEEF STOCK
BEEF STOCK
BEEF STOCK

Quadrille, Penguin Random House UK,
One Embassy Gardens, 8 Viaduct Gardens,
London SW11 7BW

Quadrille Publishing Limited is part of the Penguin
Random House group of companies whose addresses
can be found at global.penguinrandomhouse.com

Published by Quadrille in 2026

www.penguin.co.uk

A CIP catalogue record for this book is available
from the British Library

ISBN 9781837836055
10 9 8 7 6 5 4 3 2 1

Publishing Director Sarah Lavelle
Copy Editor Sally Somers
Senior Commissioning Editor Stacey Cleworth
Head of Design Katherine Case
Designer and Art Direction Jo Murphy
at Fold Graphics
Photographer Peter Lowbridge
Food and Props Stylist Anthony Murphy and Daniel
Mayo-Evans
Production Director Stephen Lang
Production Manager Sabeena Atchia

Colour reproduction by F1

Printed in Italy by L.E.G.O. S.p.A

The authorised representative in the EEA is
Penguin Random House Ireland, Morrison Chambers,
32 Nassau Street, Dublin D02 YH68.

The Beefy Boys are Anthony Murphy, Daniel Mayo-Evans, Christian Williams and Lee Symonds. What initially started as a BBQ in a back garden in Hereford has grown into multiple restaurants, food trucks and a bestselling cookbook (*The Beefy Boys: from backyard BBQs to world-class burgers*), and a range of awards including Signature Burger and Burger Chef of the Year at the National Burger Awards, as well as being finalists 7 times at The World Burger Championships. They have also featured on TV shows including *The One Show*, *The Hidden World of Hospitality with Tom Kerridge*, *Saturday Kitchen* and *Sunday Brunch*.

Find them at **thebeefyboys.com**, on Instagram **@thebeefyboys**, or check out their madcap videos on their YouTube channel '**The Beefy Boys**'.

THE
BO
Frank
BARBE